A Little Bird Told Me

A Little Bird Told Me

A collection of fascinating
facts about birds

Dominic Couzens

First published in Great Britain in 2025 by Gaia, an imprint of
Octopus Publishing Group Ltd
Carmelite House
50 Victoria Embankment
London EC4Y 0DZ
www.octopusbooks.co.uk

An Hachette UK Company
www.hachette.co.uk

The authorized representative in the EEA is Hachette Ireland,
8 Castlecourt Centre, Dublin 15, D15 XTP3, Ireland (email: info@hbgi.ie)

Text copyright © Dominic Couzens 2025
Illustrations copyright © Nancy Chiu 2025

ISBN 978-1-85675-537-5
eISBN 978-1-85675-536-8

A CIP catalogue record for this book is available from the British Library.

Typeset in 11/14pt Mrs Eaves OT by Six Red Marbles, Milton Keynes.

Printed and bound in Great Britain.

3 5 7 9 10 8 6 4 2

Commissioning Editor: Jessica Minocha
Creative Director: Mel Four
Illustrator: Nancy Chiu
Editor: Scarlet Furness
Copy Editor: Sonya Newland
Production Controller: Sarah Parry

This FSC® label means that materials used for
the product have been responsibly sourced.

For all licensed Products sold by Octopus Publishing Group Limited,
Octopus Publishing Group Limited will donate a minimum of £4,000
through an Advance and Royalty payments to RSPB Sales Ltd, which
gives all its distributable profits through Gift Aid to the RSPB.

ABOUT THE RSPB

The RSPB is the UK's largest nature conservation charity, working locally in the UK and around the world. The RSPB's vision is a shared world where wildlife, wild places and all people thrive. Their work aims to protect and restore habitats, save species, share knowledge, connect people with nature and help to end the nature and climate emergency.

'Nature is in crisis. Together we can save it.'

ABOUT THE AUTHOR

Dominic Couzens is one of the UK's leading nature writers, with more than 50 published books to his name. He is author of the best-selling *The Secret Lives of Garden Birds*, *A Year of Birdsong* and the *Great British Birdwatcher's Puzzle Book*, and has written books about mammals, insects, trees and (non-avian) dinosaurs, as well as birds. His books have sold all over the world and been translated into ten languages. He has been a leading columnist in *Bird Watching* magazine for 30 years, and in the RSPB magazine for more than 20 years. In 2021 he was awarded the Dilys Breese Medal by the British Trust for Ornithology for outstanding communication about BTO science, and in 2025 his book *An Insect a Day* was longlisted for the Wainwright Nature Writing Prize. His occasional forays into TV have included being hit over the head with a plastic truncheon by the comedian Harry Hill.

A Little Bird Told Me

THE TWELVE DAYS
OF CHRISTMAS

We all know the words to the famous Christmas tune, but what about the birds that feature in the lyrics? What exactly are calling birds? And why was there a partridge in a pear tree?

TWELVE DRUMMERS DRUMMING

There might not be any woodpeckers in the song, but we can't talk about drumming without mentioning woodpeckers. Instead of singing like other birds, they drum their bills against trees to mark their territory and attract mates! Green woodpeckers, though, hardly ever drum, preferring instead to make a call known as a 'yaffle'.

ELEVEN PIPERS PIPING

Although this line refers to the eleven faithful apostles, have you ever heard a bird call that could be described as piping? Well if you ever hear the call of a redshank on a wetland, you'll hear that piping sound that rings out across the landscape.

TEN LORDS A-LEAPING

'Ten lords a-leaping' is a reference to the biblical Ten Commandments, but when I hear about leaping, I can only think of razorbill and guillemot chicks. Before leaving their clifftop nests, they have to take a huge leap of faith, leaping off the ledge and dropping to the safety of the sea below. At this life stage, ready to jump, they are known as jumplings.

NINE LADIES DANCING

Worthy of a spot in the *Strictly Come Dancing* final, the courtship dance of the great crested grebe is one of nature's great spectacles. Two birds will shake their heads, synchronously moving their fancy plumes from side to side, then rear out of the water in a stunning display. Grebes don't feature in the song, but they deserve a mention for their extravagant performance!

EIGHT MAIDS A-MILKING

Did you know that woodpigeons are able to produce a kind of milk, known as 'crop milk'? This allows them to feed their chicks exclusively with milk for the first few days of their lives. This extraordinary ability also means that as long as there is an abundance of food, pigeons can breed at any time of year. The only other birds to produce crop milk are flamingos and the emperor penguin.

SEVEN SWANS A-SWIMMING

Alongside the iconic mute swan that we see in ponds and Royal Parks around the UK, two other species come to visit for Christmas. Whooper and Bewick's swans migrate from Arctic regions and can be spotted feeding on farmland, estuaries and freshwater lakes throughout autumn and winter. You can identify them by their beak; Bewick's have a rounded yellow patch, while the whooper's looks like a wedge of yellow cheese!

SIX GEESE A-LAYING

According to the Bible, it took six days to create the world and it is believed that this is exactly what the six geese a-laying represent!

FIVE GOLD RINGS

This line has several bird-related theories. The first is that the gold rings refer to the rings around the neck of a pheasant, but as the pheasant's rings are white, I'm not convinced! Another theory is that lyric was supposed to be 'goldspinks', the old name for goldfinches, which were commonly kept as caged pets, although less so since taking them from the wild was made illegal.

FOUR CALLING BIRDS

This part of the song is a story in two halves. The number four is said to represent the Gospels. But in the Old English version of the song, the words were 'four colly birds' – colly being the name of a dark-coloured bird with a beautiful song, or what we now know as blackbirds.

THREE FRENCH HENS

It is said that the three French hens represent the three virtues: hope, faith and love. Hens would have once been a highly prized meat on a festive dining table, and French hens could have been a luxury import in the 16th century!

TWO TURTLE DOVES

Doves are a traditional festive image, but in this instance I think the two turtle doves were put into the song to represent peace, which they are traditionally believed to bring. Oddly, turtle doves are summer visitors to Britain and not around at Christmas.

AND A PARTRIDGE IN A PEAR TREE

This ground-dwelling bird that heads up the song is the focus of many theories, including that the partridge in the tree represents Christ's body on the cross. (Incidentally, the French name for a partridge is *perdrix* – which sounds very like 'pear tree'.)

FAVOURITE BIRD FACTS:
MUTE SWAN

- There is no such thing as a 'swansong'. The words
  come from the mistaken belief that swans, silent
  for most of their life, sing a beautiful song just
  before expiring. They don't though – they're more
  likely to murmur an expletive!
- Cygnets are usually expelled from the family
  territory in the autumn. They join non-breeding
  flocks of similar-aged birds, where they learn
  about life until they start to breed at around the
  age of three.
- The mute swan's aggressive display, in which it
  ruffles its back feathers and swims forward, is
  known as 'busking'.

CHRISTMAS
FAMILY HOLIDAYS

A lot of British bird species are seasoned travellers, touching many parts of the globe and flying unimaginable distances. Let's have a look at some of those remarkable journeys.

Many geese come to the UK from the Arctic in winter and, unusually, most species migrate in parties. Most migratory birds don't travel with parents.

Breeding male goosanders take a 'lads' holiday' to Arctic Norway and Sweden for a moult after the breeding season.

Curlew sandpiper males may remain on their Arctic breeding grounds for an incredibly short time, as little as two weeks – which is just enough for a few casual flings!

Cuckoos are usually the first bird to leave the UK after breeding. They may arrive in April and depart in June, leaving their offspring behind to be looked after by their foster families.

When migrating, house martins sometimes roost in unoccupied nests when they're on their way south from their breeding grounds – effectively a bird Airbnb!

Have you ever climbed a mountain? A treecreeper has! Well, not technically, but if you add up all the creeping up and down that a treecreeper does in a single day, it roughly corresponds to climbing Ben Nevis (1,345m/4,413ft).

Some birds will double their body weight before migration to give them the energy needed for those long, sometimes even non-stop flights. Can we use that excuse during Christmas dinner?

Swifts make one of the longest migrations of any bird, travelling an average of 22,530km (14,000 miles) every year to and from equatorial and southern Africa. They fly through the airspace of 25 countries en route.

Blackcaps have altered their migration path. Rather than going north to south, some now fly east to west, spending winters in the UK, taking advantage of the food that humans leave out in the garden feeders.

Once they've left the nest, young swifts will not land again for roughly two years, until they themselves have young! They can essentially switch off half their brain to allow that side to rest, while remaining airborne.

Whooper swans are some of the highest-flying migrant species. Airline pilots have clocked them at 8,850m (29,035ft).

Whooper swans are also champion long-distance fliers. They can make it from Iceland to Scotland in one go – that's more than 820km (510 miles) without a service-station break!

The Arctic tern is justifiably famous for its migration, sometimes travelling up to 90,000km (56,000 miles) annually. In fact, if an Arctic tern lived for 35 years, it would fly the equivalent of three trips around the Moon!

The bar-tailed godwit undertakes the longest non-stop migration of any land bird, flying each year from Alaska to New Zealand or Australia. In 2023, one hardy member of this species was recorded flying from Alaska to Tasmania, covering a barely believable 13,560km (8,426 miles) without stopping. It took just 11 days.

An iconic summer visitor, swallows are well known for their migration. In spring, they can travel over 300km (186 miles) per day!

Swallows usually migrate by day, but once they reach the Sahara on their way to their wintering grounds, they switch to night-flight mode.

FAVOURITE BIRD FACTS: GREY HERON

- Grey herons are often spotted simply standing in fields, looking characteristically fed up. A study from a day roost in Yorkshire found that an individual may spend 77 per cent of daylight hours doing nothing at all – not even sleeping. This might explain a recent drive to recruit herons for jobs in the civil service . . .
- There are lots of excellent places in marshes and wetlands for safe nesting. So where do herons place their colonies? In the treetops!

DO THEY KNOW
IT'S CHRISTMAS?

It's cold outside, and quite a few of the birds that spent the summer with us are now far away, passing the winter in more comfortable climates. Let's take a look at where some UK breeding birds spend the winter months.

Swift: Over central and southern Africa, sometimes even reaching the east coast of Africa in Mozambique, high aloft.

Swallow: As far as the Cape region of South Africa – they could be flying over elephants in transit after spending the summer in the UK.

Cuckoo: The Congolese forests, sharing their habitat with gorillas and bonobos!

Turtle dove: The Sahel region of Africa, just south of the Sahara – maybe flying over Timbuktu.

Manx shearwater: Off southern South America, sharing the sea with albatrosses.

Arctic tern: The icy waters around Antarctica, chasing the same fish as penguins after a summer by the British seaside.

Kittiwake: Over the waters of the western Atlantic (especially first-years) and far offshore, riding the storms.

Puffin: Immersed in the North Sea or the Atlantic Ocean, far from land.

Lesser whitethroat: Eastern Africa, resting in acacia trees that are being nibbled by giraffes.

Common whitethroat: West Africa, south of the Sahara, with the sun on their backs.

Osprey: Coastal West Africa, enjoying the beach life!

Blackcap: Southern Spain, among the olive groves.

Ring ouzel: North African highlands, among the juniper trees.

Goldfinch: France or Spain, for a spot of midwinter sun.

FAVOURITE BIRD FACTS:
CORMORANT

- Cormorants often swallow pebbles and other hard objects in order to reduce their buoyancy for diving. Natural selection ensures that they don't swallow too many.
- Experts claim that cormorants hold their wings out to dry, but nobody has ever disproved the notion that they could be telling other cormorants the size of their previous catch!
- Despite their size, cormorants can fly very well and can soar to great heights.

PUTTING THE
PIECES TOGETHER

With more than 10,000 species of birds around the world, there's a lot of anatomical variety! Here are some of the most curious anatomical features of British birds.

Did you know that most birds don't have penises? Instead, males and females have a single internal chamber called the cloaca. Of course, there are exceptions to this rule. Male mallards are among the 3 per cent of bird species that do have a penis. In fact, they're well known for their unique, corkscrew-shaped appendage!

Ruffs are well known for their changing plumage, making it tricky to identify them. But another fun fact about ruffs is that, in spring, the male bird's testes are actually heavier than its brain!

Birds don't have bladders. Scientists believe that this is to keep them light during flight. Instead of urine as we know it, birds excrete a pasty white substance.

The feral pigeon has extraordinary abilities, including being able to hear infrasound, detecting changes in atmospheric pressure, and homing. Think of that next time you see a pigeon feasting on spilt chips in a city centre.

Do you know how to tell the difference between a male and a female starling? Look at the base of the bill. This is blue in the male and pink in the female.

In a study of European coal tits, it was found that Norwegian coal tits have longer sperm than their German counterparts!

The sperm of barn swallows breeding near the Chernobyl radiation zone showed abnormal morphology when compared to that of barn swallows breeding in other areas.

The grey heron, a dinosaurish-looking bird, has specially elongated neck vertebrae. These make a hinge that enables the heron to 'snap' towards a fish in the water below it.

Cormorants' feathers don't produce the same 'water-proofing' substance that other seabirds have. That's why you might spot them sitting with their wings outstretched, drying them out and looking like tiny dragons on the sea!

Cranes have such a long trachea to amplify the sound of their trumpeting call that it winds around the sternum. They make quite a racket when groups come in to roost across the fens!

Stone-curlews are part of a family called 'thick-knees'. The name doesn't actually refer to the knee, but rather to the tibiotarsal joint – an ankle equivalent. Maybe they should be called 'thick-ankles' instead!

Sea ducks are among the record holders for diving depths. In fact, long-tailed ducks can dive down as far as 60m (197ft) in search of food sources such as molluscs, small fish and fish eggs.

The tip of the sanderling's bill is so sensitive that it can detect the movement of its prey in wet sand without touching it. As it immerses its bill and displaces water, the waves bounce off a solid object and reflect back. The sanderling's bill detects this, a bit like echolocation.

Many birds have special visual adaptations, but the kingfisher has a particularly clever ocular feature. Its eyes change to binocular vision as it tilts its head downward, allowing it to get the best view of potential dinner items.

Woodcocks' eyes are positioned so far back on their head that they have almost 360-degree vision! This adaptation helps them to detect predators while they're feeding, but it does mean their eyesight isn't great when looking forward.

Bird calls and songs are produced by an organ called the syrinx, which is at the junction of the bronchi and trachea. A lot of birdsong is the composite of two airflows.

The snipe has the longest bill relative to its size of any British bird.

Barn owls have asymmetrical ear openings. The left ear is higher than the right, enabling the owls to hear in three dimensions and hunt in complete darkness.

The crossbill is the only bird that has crossed mandibles, which develop around 20 days after the bird is born. The lower mandible either crosses to the right or left of the upper mandible. Around 50 per cent of the birds are left-billed and 50 per cent are right-billed.

A gannet's nostrils are internal, to prevent water getting up its nose under pressure and exploding its brain as it hits the water at 190km/h (118mph).

ROCKIN' ROBINS

We couldn't have a Christmas book about birds
without mentioning the most iconic star of Christmas
cards around the world, could we? But how much
do you know about robin red breast?

Robins are small birds, with a wingspan of just 20–22cm (8–8.7in).

Only adult robins have the red/orange breast. Youngsters have brown speckled chests until they reach maturity.

The robin's diet is made up of fruit, seeds and insects. You will often see robins on your garden bird tables.

Female robins build nests low to the ground using moss, dead leaves and even hair. They have been known to nest in unusual places, including wellies and plant pots!

The robin didn't become a symbol of Christmas until the Victorian period, when postmen – who wore red waistcoats – were nicknamed 'robins'. The birds started to appear on Christmas cards as a tribute to the postmen who delivered them. Before that, robins were actually called 'redbreasts'.

Robins are hugely territorial and will fight to the death if it means keeping their patch safe. Don't cross a robin!

Robins hunt by taking a high perch and watching for the movement of invertebrates below. That's why you'll often see them perching on garden tools like spades.

Robins often pair up in December. However, they don't start breeding until March at the earliest, so this is rather like an 'engagement' period.

FAVOURITE BIRD FACTS:
SPARROWHAWK

- Sparrowhawks are stealth attackers that sometimes use a screen to approach target birds. They have been known to flip over garden fences, use hanging laundry, or creep up on birds from behind people.
- Sparrowhawks breed comparatively late in the year so that they can feed their young on fledgling birds, which are inexperienced and easy to catch.

- If you see a sparrowhawk with a collared dove or a woodpigeon, it will always be a female. Female sparrowhawks are typically almost twice as heavy as males, and also slightly longer, and aren't as good as males at catching small, mobile prey. They are better at handling larger food items such as pigeons and doves.

DO YOU HEAR WHAT I HEAR?

*Birdsong can be heard everywhere — from the
open countryside to the heart of a busy city — and
different species each have their own genre of music.
Which is your favourite?*

Ay-up! Experiments with chaffinches have revealed that males learn their songs from their father and his neighbours, and they often exhibit local dialects. There might be a Yorkshire chaffinch!

Research has shown that listening to birdsong can transform mental health and offer relief from mental fatigue. So, open your window and listen to the sounds of nature to lift your spirits.

Some birds sing notes that are so high that humans can't hear them – a bit like Mariah Carey's whistle at the end of 'All I Want for Christmas Is You'!

Okay, I promised you birdsong, but let's spend a moment on mute swans. They get their name from their lack of call while in flight. Swans and geese are usually known for their noisy calls as they fly overhead, but the mechanical sound you hear from a mute swan is actually made by its wings.

The mute swan's cousin, the whooper swan, makes a whooping, trumpeting racket both on the ground and as it takes to the sky.

The brilliant white, blue-eyed gannet, often seen over cliffs around the UK coastline, makes a distinctive sound reminiscent of someone blowing through a cane, a bit like a didgeridoo!

A study at the University of St Andrews found that tawny owls don't sing as much in the rain as they do when it's dry, as their calls get drowned out by the sound of the downpour. You could say that it's literally too wet to woo.

In terms of singing stamina, woodlarks come high on the list. One individual has been recorded singing for 96 minutes non-stop. That's almost as long as a West End musical!

The booming bittern has a far-carrying note that may be the lowest-pitched call of any British bird! The deep 'boom' can carry for at least 2km (1.2 miles).

The spoonbill is almost completely silent, although you may occasionally hear that spoon-shaped bill snapping shut!

Know anyone that talks a lot? They'd get on well with the yellowhammer, which can sing up to 7,000 times a day in the summer months. True performers . . .

Little egrets are part of the heron family, but their call is certainly unique. They sound just like they're blowing bubbles underwater.

Ever heard a black and white coastal bird singing 'peep peep'? That will be an oystercatcher. A group of oystercatchers makes one of the loudest sounds of any bird species.

The chiffchaff's scientific name, *collybita*, comes from the Greek for 'money-changer'. The tones of the chiffs and chaffs correspond to different-sized coins.

The trilling song of the wren contains over 100 different notes. Try and count them next time you hear a wren singing in a hedgerow.

FAVOURITE BIRD FACTS:
MOORHEN

- Moorhens don't live on moors. The name derives from 'mere-hen', a 'mere' being a shallow lake or wetland.
- Next time you see a moorhen, look for the red patch at the top of the legs.
- Moorhens may have several broods a year. Helpful offspring from a previous brood often take a turn feeding the later chicks of the season.

CHRISTMAS CAROLLERS

It's the middle of winter, but some birds have already started singing. Song is stimulated by increasing day length, which means that many birds begin after the winter solstice on 21/22 December. But on Christmas Day you might hear some of the following songsters.

Robin (all the time)
Wren (a lot)
Dunnock (still, sunny mornings)
Song thrush (mornings, often when dark)
Mistle thrush (intermittent)
Great tit (will soon be a dominant sound)
Coal tit (more localised, usually from conifers)
Dipper (rare, around rushing streams)
Cetti's warbler (rare, around marshes)
Goldfinch (gardens, usually on sunny days)

What's your favourite birdsong to brighten the chilly winter days?

ALL TOGETHER NOW

*A flamboyance of flamingos . . . a tower of giraffes . . . a troop
of baboons . . . Collective nouns for animals are a favourite
for lots of people, and some of them date back as far as the
15th century. How many of these have you heard of?*

A bouquet of avocets
A siege of bitterns
A cloud of blackbirds
A confusion of chiffchaffs
A chattering of choughs
A commotion of coots
A gulp of cormorants
A murder of crows
A caravan of cranes
A stand of curlews
A trip of dotterels
A fling of dunlins
A charm of finches

A gaggle of geese (but a skein of geese when in flight)
A brood of grouse
A sedge of herons
A clattering of jackdaws
A scold of jays
A coterie of kingfishers
A hovering of kestrels
A parliament of owls
A bouquet of pheasants
A plump of pigeons
A circus of puffins
An unkindness of ravens
A round of robins
A host of sparrows
A murmuration of starlings
A flight of swallows
A lamentation of swans
A colony of terns
A descent of woodpeckers

NAUGHTY OR NICE?

*The behaviour of some birds would definitely
earn them a place on the 'naughty' list . . .*

Male pied flycatchers aren't always the most faithful mates.
While a female is sitting on the eggs, the male might form
another territory, up to 2km (1.2 miles) away, and pair up
with a second mate. He'll leave her when the eggs of his
primary mate hatch.

Male capercaillie get very angry during the mating season
in spring. They'll attack anything that moves, including
deer, cyclists and people with cameras!

Goldeneye nest in holes – but that's not all. Females often
dump eggs in their neighbour's nests to boost their own
productivity.

Often lacking their own interior design ideas, shags and cormorants are particularly prone to stealing nest material from other birds in preparation for nesting season.

Moorhen often lay their eggs in the nests of other moorhens and even those of other species, such as coots.

Tawny owls are fiercely competitive, and have even been known to kill their own offspring in autumn if they end up competing for territory – which seems somewhat counterproductive!

Bittern breeding season is a dangerous time, with males fighting to the death over females.

Adult coots will kill their young if they think there are too many in the brood. (Maybe because a moorhen left its eggs in their nest!) They also 'split' broods, with the male and female each taking responsibility for a share in an admirable act of co-parenting!

Blackbirds sometimes wait until a song thrush has broken a snail's shell before swooping in and stealing the snail for themselves. Lazy or innovative? You decide!

A little owl once committed murder, killing its mate and then feeding it to its chicks. It must have been desperate to ensure the survival of its offspring!

A single male corn bunting once paired up with 18 females in a single season!

FAVOURITE BIRD FACTS: CUCKOO

- One of the earliest, pioneering studies of the cuckoo's brood parasitism was undertaken by none other than Edward Jenner, inventor of the smallpox vaccine.
- The cuckoo is one of the few British birds that can eat caterpillars with noxious hairs. It gobbles them down with impunity.
- A female cuckoo raised by a pair of reed warblers, meadow pipits, dunnocks or robins will go on to be a brood parasite of the species that fostered it.

- Legend has it that when you hear the first cuckoo of spring, the number of 'cuckoo' repetitions it makes is the number of years you have left in your life.

STATISTICS CORNER

Time to crunch some numbers . . .

6,000,000: The number of starlings in the largest ever murmuration, recorded in Somerset.

2,400,000: The average number of kilometres (1,500,000 miles) travelled by an Arctic tern in its lifetime.

18: The weight in kilos (40lb) that a great bustard can reach, making it the heaviest flying bird.

140,000: The most red knots ever recorded at the RSPB Snettisham 'wader spectacular'.

60: The depth in metres (197ft) that a puffin can dive in search of dinner.

322: The speed in kilometres per hour (200mph) of a diving peregrine falcon.

100: The number of caterpillars that a young blue tit can eat in a single day.

11: The number of eggs that a capercaillie can lay in a single nesting season.

167: The weight in grams (6oz) of the average jay.

700,000: The number of yellowhammer breeding territories that have been recorded across the UK.

FAVOURITE BIRD FACTS:
TAWNY OWL

- The eyes of the tawny owl are the same size as ours. However, they are more sensitive, so an owl's image is 2.7 times brighter than that of a human in the same light intensity.
- Owls are not especially wise, I just think they look intelligent because their forward-facing eyes and round faces resemble ours!
- Owls have almost silent flight. Their flight feathers are softened and the leading edges have a comb-like structure, which reduces turbulence.

- Owls fly slowly, so if they do hit something in flight, the impact speed is low.

WHEN A CHILD IS BORN

*From the cute to the strange, bird families
are both diverse and wonderful.*

Herring gull chicks are truly resourceful – so much so that they have been known to 'fire' their parents if they don't provide enough food. The chicks will then take their chances in the next-door nest, hoping to be adopted.

The great crested grebe is one of few birds in which the young ride on an adult's back. Others include the mute swan, goosander, red-breasted merganser and tufted duck.

Long-tailed tit young are the only small birds to spend Christmas with their parents!

Common sandpiper pairs each make a nest scrape and show them to each other, presumably deciding which one is best for their offspring.

In a clutch of four common sandpiper eggs, the last one may not hatch until sixteen hours after the first. That's a long wait for the parents!

Purple sandpipers protect their nests by impersonating a rodent – crouching, running and squeaking at attackers.

In a reversal of typical bird behaviour, female dotterels initiate mating displays and males rear the chicks.

In another role reversal, a black-tailed godwit female leaves the male with incubation duties.

Blue tits have the greatest range of clutch size of any small bird, laying anywhere between three and twenty-two eggs.

In the spring, adult bullfinches develop a 'pouch' on the side of their palate, in which they store food to feed their young.

INSALUBRIOUS HABITS

With such a huge variety of bird species in the UK alone, it's no surprise to discover that some of them have downright disgusting habits!

Brent geese create an unpleasant mess at dinner time – they're reputed to poo every three minutes when feeding!

Fulmars, whose name means 'foul gull' in Old Norse, create a nasty-smelling oil that they store in their stomachs, which they'll squirt on anything that disturbs them in their nest. The kicker? It doesn't wash off!

Red kites are scavengers, feasting on the bodies of dead animals. These birds famously hung around the executioner's block in medieval times, to pick at the corpses of criminals who died by the axe.

Curlews have always been a bad omen to sailors, who once believed that hearing a curlew calling at night foreshadowed bad luck.

White storks are often depicted delivering babies to happy new parents. However, some storks kill their chicks to secure the survival of other offspring, so perhaps we shouldn't trust them to deliver our own!

Hoopoes are famous for their foul-smelling excretions. From the safety of their malodorous nests, hoopoe young fire faeces at intruders with great accuracy.

Victorians would poke out the eyes of their pet linnets with needles, believing that this made them sing more sweetly.

The Latin name for the nightjar means 'goat sucker'. They got the name because, according to Pliny the Elder, these birds fed on milk directly from goats at night, turning the milk sour.

FAVOURITE BIRD FACTS:
BLACKBIRD

- The song of a blackbird gets more complex with age. An individual's breeding success also increases with age.
- You can tell a male blackbird's state of health by the colour of its bill. The more orange it is, the healthier the bird.
- Divorce among blackbirds is most frequent in low-quality breeding habitats.
- Blackbirds practise singing gently in midwinter, 'under the breath' with the bill closed. This is known as 'subsong'.

CHRISTMAS JUMPERS

I hope that you found a new jumper under the
Christmas tree, to swap for your old plumage!
Here are some facts about how birds cover up.

Male mallards moult in summer, losing their shiny green head feathers to look more like the female of the species.

Honey-buzzards are an unusual bird of prey, feeding on the nests and larvae of wasps and bees. Their unusually tight plumage prevents stings from penetrating to the skin while they're eating.

Ptarmigans are well adapted to the snowy conditions that are common in their habitat, with their thick feet feathers acting like snow shoes. They also experience three moults per year, allowing them to blend in with the changing mountain scenery.

Grey herons have 'powder down' – feathers that are permanently breaking down into a fine powder. They help absorb any fish oils that may get on to the feathers during feeding, which would inhibit flight.

Think kingfishers are blue? Think again. Their iridescent feathers are actually colourless. The blue colour they are known for occurs through a phenomenon called structural colouration.

The yellow on the plumage of a blue tit varies between individuals, and is related to the number of caterpillars they ate during the moult.

FAVOURITE BIRD FACTS:
NIGHTINGALE

- The nightingale is a summer visitor, so if you hear a bird at night in winter it isn't a nightingale.
- The song of the nightingale may have 1,000 different elements, or phrases, making it one of the most complex birdsongs in the world.
- Nightingales sing by day as well as night. Day song is for repelling males; night song is said to entice migrating females.

- The poem 'Ode to a Nightingale' was written by John Keats in 1819. It was a particularly good year for nightingales on Hampstead Heath, near where Keats lived. They are long gone from the area now.

THROUGH THE AGES

*Birds are ancient creatures, having been around
for at least 150 million years. Let's have a look at
some standout moments for birds through the ages.*

Birds were a popular pet in Victorian times. Usually, those who lived in small houses chose wild birds such as wrens and jackdaws as pets.

During the reign of Henry VIII, the windows of Hampton Court were adorned with ornamental bird cages that contained nightingales and canaries.

Rome may never have expanded into its great empire had it not been for a gaggle of greylag geese. In 390 BC, a night-time attack went undetected by soldiers and guard dogs, but the greylags – the sacred animal of the god Juno – were startled and their honks raised the alarm.

Avocets were hunted to extinction during the Victoria era. Their return to our shores is attributed to the flooding of coastal marshes to create sea defences during the First World War, which established the perfect habitat for them to recolonise.

Henry VIII is thought to be partially responsible for a severe decline in the populations of many bird species. The Preservation of Grain Act of 1532 encouraged people to kill any birds on a list of 'vermin' species thought to be spreading disease that was causing bad harvests. Rewards were given for the head of a red kite or a rook. Interestingly, many of the species on that list are now priority species to protect.

'If the ravens leave the tower, the kingdom shall fall.' No one knows the exact origins of the legend of the ravens in the Tower of London, but it's thought that Charles II protected them after being advised that if they left, London would crumble. The ravens can still be seen at the Tower today.

During the medieval period, people believed that goldfinches could protect them from bubonic plague. Leonardo da Vinci observed goldfinches turning their heads away from sick individuals and took that as a predictor that the person would succumb to the plague.

In the 19th century, working-class families ate goose at Christmas rather than turkey, and 'Goose Clubs' were set up to help people save money for a Christmas goose. Households who could not afford a goose may have eaten chicken or even pigeon.

During the Second World War, around 250,000 pigeons were used to deliver messages to the troops. One pigeon, named GI Joe, saved the lives of 1,000 British troops when he delivered a message from an Italian village that was scheduled to be attacked!

A wooden falcon bought for £75 at auction was later identified as the emblem of Anne Boleyn that would likely have decorated her private apartment. The sculpture, thought to be worth over £200,000, is now on permanent loan to Hampton Court Palace.

The word 'orange' wasn't used until the 16th century, when the fruit of the same name was first imported. Before that, red was the closest colour so things that were actually orange – the robin's red breast, the red kite and the redstart, for example – were known as 'red' and the name stuck.

Kingfishers, a much-loved species today, were one of the most hunted bird species during the Tudor period.

The Tudors were the first to eat turkey as part of their Christmas dinner, although they were just one of several types of bird that made up a festive banquet. These North American birds remained an exclusively upper-class dish until after the Second World War, when they became cheaper to rear.

FAVOURITE BIRD FACTS:
MAGPIE

- There are two strata to magpie society: those that are paired up have a territory, while the non-breeding flock does not. There is much tension between the haves and the have-nots!
- In spring, magpies form ceremonial gatherings, in which a pair is challenged by a bird that wants their territory. All the local magpies gather around to noisily watch the skirmish.

- The female magpie 'knows' how many eggs to lay. It makes an assessment of how abundant food is within its territory and lays its clutch accordingly.

CHRISTMAS DINNER

Looking forward to your Christmas dinner? To get you in the mood, here are some fun feeding facts about birds.

In the Catholic religion, no meat is supposed to be consumed on a Friday. To get around this, many bird species, including barnacle geese, were reclassified as seafood in Ireland! (In the USA, beavers were also classed as a fish.)

White-fronted geese can be found feeding in large family flocks made up of several generations that migrate together to their feeding grounds.

The Ross's gull, which inhabits Arctic regions, feeds on insects in summer but changes its diet completely in winter, to feed on plankton.

Treecreepers eat more spiders than most other small birds.

Willow tits are said to need to eat something every 2.5 seconds in midwinter in order to maintain their condition.

Shovelers have an advanced filter-feeding system. They work together, moving in large circles, with one bird following the other to use mud kicked up by the bird in front to filter food.

Wigeons are grazers, with around 80 per cent of their diet made up of grass.

Capercaillie prefer a spiky diet and spend the winter eating pine needles.

Leach's petrels eat very small planktonic items.

Plump ptarmigans are not at all fussy when it comes to food. They can even be found eating twigs!

Cormorants are usually first to the seafood buffet, and can acquire all the food they need for the whole day in about half an hour.

Turnstones are so called because of their behaviour, flipping over stones in search of food. They'll eat anything – from chips to aquatic insects. They have even been recorded eating soap!

Unlike most other waders, greenshanks eat quite a lot of fish, which they pick out from shallow waters, along with small invertebrates.

Little auk, cousins of the extinct great auk, are the only British seabird to prey principally on copepods – small crustaceans found in both fresh and salt water.

Great grey shrikes are 'butcher birds', impaling edible items on thorns, sharp sticks or even barbed wire. Being truly carnivorous, they also eat small mammals and other birds.

Beautiful waxwings are Europe's only true frugivore, and can consume close to 1,000 berries a day!

Woodlarks and skylarks have a curious habit of collecting insects and putting them in a pile, before gathering them up and taking them to their young.

A pair of blue tits can collect 1,000 caterpillars a day to feed their hungry young. They break the jaws of larger caterpillars to prevent them from biting.

FAVOURITE BIRD FACTS: SWALLOW

- Female swallows select a mate based on the length and symmetry of his tail streamers. The longer and more symmetrical the better.
- Male swallows have a delightful song, but sometimes intersperse little buzzes, which are territorial signals.
- Swallows eat larger flying insects than house martins do, and fly lower to catch them.

BIRDS OF PREY

The UK is home to 15 species of birds of prey, and each one has its own unique and fascinating qualities.

Have you ever seen a buzzard standing in a field as you drive past? These birds often hunt simply by walking over muddy ground, looking for worms.

A golden eagle's size means it can fly in high wind and stormy weather. In fact, the turbulence often helps it on its way.

Female sparrowhawks are much larger and heavier than the males. They often hunt different food, preventing competition between sexes.

Hen harriers are true performance artists, with an amazing sky-dance display that males engage in to impress females.

Like their wizard namesake, merlins use trickery and deception to catch their food, adopting the undulating flight of a thrush to conceal their approach.

The hobby is a talented stealth hunter, able to catch even speedy swifts and bats.

Marsh harriers have an impressive food-passing display, in which a male drops food into the waiting talons of a female that has flipped upside down to catch it!

The UK is home to the fourth-largest eagle in the world. The white-tailed eagle, which can be spotted in parts of Scotland and the south coast of England, has a wingspan of up to 2.4m (7.9ft).

Golden eagles often hunt in pairs, working together with one member flushing and the other catching the prey.

Hobbies nest very late in the season in order to take advantage of an abundance of young birds with relatively limited flying skills.

FAVOURITE BIRD FACTS: BLUE TIT

- The blue tit's cap and other blue parts of its plumage have strong ultraviolet reflectance. Birds with similar UV reflectance tend to pair up.
- Blue tits time their breeding to coincide with the spring glut of moths.

WHAT'S IN A NAME?

Some bird names just make sense — blackbird, for example — but others need a bit more work to decipher . . .

The name of the cirl bunting derives from the Italian *zirlare*, which means to chirp or sing.

The alternative name for the little grebe, dabchick, means 'dive chick'.

Whinchats are another strangely named bird. 'Whin' is an old name for gorse. Whinchats aren't gorse lovers, so they should probably have been named stonechat, but of course we already have that!

The name nightjar was first used around 400 years ago. The 'jar' suffix refers to the jarring noise that the bird makes.

Until the late medieval period, birds weren't even called birds – they were known as 'fowls'. Chaucer's poem 'The Parliament of Fowls' refers to this. The Saxon word 'bird' referred to chicks and young fowls. 'Fowl' was still the popular usage for large birds such as corvids, while 'bird' remained the way to refer to small birds.

The name of the hobby comes from the Old French word *hober*, which means to jump around, in reference to the birds' aerial display.

The cuckoo is named after its two-note call – as is the chiffchaff.

The scientific name of the long-eared owl is *Asio otus*, while until recently the scientific name of the eastern screech owl, found in North America, was the reverse – *Otus asio*. The latter has now been changed to *Megascops asio*.

The French name for the eider is *Eider à duvet*.

Very rarely, bird genera and plant genera are the same. So, you might see a dunnock (*Prunella modularis*) while standing on self heal (*Prunella vulgaris*). You might spot a northern wheatear (*Oenanthe oenanthe*) while walking next to some hemlock water-dropwort (*Oenanthe crocata*), a common waterside plant.

Less likely, you might watch a northern gannet (*Morus bassanus*) flying offshore while sheltering under a white mulberry tree (*Morus alba*).

Excluding the catch-all 'American', there are more British birds named after Egypt than any other country – Egyptian goose, Egyptian nightjar and Egyptian vulture.

Three birds on the British List are named after Kent or places in Kent: Kentish plover, Dartford warbler and Sandwich tern.

The skylark and its immediate kin are the only birds in the world named after the sky – which is odd, considering that they live mainly on the ground!

The lesser spotted . . . lesser spotted! There are only two birds in the world with 'lesser spotted' in their name. One of them is our own lesser spotted woodpecker; the other is the Eurasian lesser spotted eagle.

The Italian name for the magpie is *gazza*, the same as the nickname given to the playmaker of English football in the 1980s and 1990s, Paul Gascoigne. Coincidentally, he began his career playing for Newcastle United, 'The Magpies', and for a while played for Italian club Lazio.

COUNTING CROWS

Corvids are a big part of everyday life in the UK, from the screeching jay as we walk through the woods, to the rooks nesting above the workplace. Corvids are an extremely intelligent group of birds, so I thought they deserved a section all of their own.

Jays are famous for storing large numbers of acorns. In fact, a pair of jays may collect and store 3,000–5,000 acorns in the autumn. Retrieving them requires extraordinary feats of memory – could you remember where you left something a few months ago?

Magpies are known to have awareness of self, and can recognise themselves in a mirror.

If you listen to a chough, it sounds like it's saying 'cheo-ow'. So should they be called cheoows instead?

Jackdaws were once a common pet, and they may have been able to learn some words from their owners. Ravens and jackdaws are known to mimic sounds from their environment, so this is not beyond the realms of possibility.

Jackdaws are among the most faithful British birds. Their divorce rate is almost zero!

Rooks are early nesters, often with eggs in March. It is possible that they nest early to ensure the ground isn't to dry to dig for worms when the young hatch.

Jackdaws lay eggs at intervals, so their chicks are different ages. If food sources are abundant, most of the chicks will survive, but if there's a lack of food only the oldest usually makes it to fledge.

Some rook colonies may have been in same place since the Middle Ages.

The expression 'as the crow flies' actually refers to rooks. At the time it was coined, people would not have made a distinction between rooks and crows, and would have been familiar with the lines of birds flying between feeding areas and roosts. For the same reason, scarecrows should really be called 'scarerooks'.

A raven named George was dismissed from his job at the Tower of London in 1986, after taking a liking to local TV antennas. He was rehoused at the Welsh Mountain Zoo.

FAVOURITE BIRD FACTS: GOLDFINCH

- The male goldfinch's bill is 10 per cent (1mm/ 0.04in) longer than the female's, on average.
- Male goldfinches are more likely to feed from teasel than are females.
- They line their nests with super-soft plant down, especially thistledown.
- The nest is built far out along a branch, often over water, for safety against ground predators such as weasels or snakes.

BIRDS IN CULTURE

*Artists, writers, composers and filmmakers all love
to incorporate birds into their work. Birds also have
significance in various religions, and can invoke
national pride in many countries. Can you remember
any birds from your childhood movies or books?*

In the *Harry Potter* books, the snowy owl that accompanies
the young hero through his years at Hogwarts is a female.
In the films, however, Hedwig is played by several male
owls, because only the males of the species have the
stark white colouring that J K Rowling described. And
here's another fun fact: snowy owls aren't a native species
in the UK!

The inventor of the football game Subbuteo wanted to call
it 'The Hobby' after the bird of prey, but he was overruled.
Instead, he gave it part of the bird's scientific name,
Falco subbuteo.

The golden eagle is the most popular national animal in the world, representing Albania, Germany, Austria, Mexico and Kazakhstan.

When you hear an owl's 'twit-twoo' in a film, you can be pretty sure that it's a sample of the male and female tawny owl's call and response, as this is the only species that makes the familiar sound.

The cheerful background noise of birdsong in films is often the call of a chaffinch. This is perhaps surprising when you consider that chaffinches are common across Europe, but less so in America, the home of Hollywood.

In the 16th and 17th centuries, goldfinches were a popular pet, so they appear in many paintings of that period, especially those featuring children.

Goldfinches also have symbolic significance in many religious artworks. The birds are said to be able to eat seeds from a thistle without injuring themselves, in the same way that Christ is said to have withstood a crown of thorns.

In the *Angry Birds* movie, the character Chuck's super speed is based on that of a peregrine falcon.

Great northern divers are seabirds with a seriously sinister call. This has been used to create a creepy atmosphere in film and TV, from *Harry Potter* to *Game of Thrones* to Thanos's woodland retreat in *Avengers: Infinity War*.

Herring gulls aren't known for flying far out into the open ocean, but their calls can be heard in the middle of the ocean in films such as *Pirates of the Caribbean*!

The mythical liver bird is the symbol of the city of Liverpool, and may have been for as much as 650 years. Originally, the bird was probably meant to be an eagle, but by the 17th century the liver bird had been reinvented and based on a cormorant.

Ralph Vaughan Williams's famous piece 'The Lark Ascending' was inspired by the song of the skylark. It is considered one of the most beautiful pieces of classical music ever written.

The song 'Sparrow', by Simon and Garfunkel, tells the story of a sparrow that is overlooked by everyone. It was written to remind people to appreciate the beauty of small things in everyday life.

A fun fact for your pub quiz: 'Eagle' is the longest ABBA song ever recorded, clocking in at five minutes!

The story of Chicken Little, who went to tell the king that the sky was falling down, is based on a European folk tradition dating back 2,500 years.

In 1989, the RSPB released a film about a heron called *Big Bill*. Have you seen it?

In *A Christmas Carol*, Bob Cratchit is scraping money together to buy a goose for his family's Christmas dinner, before Scrooge purchases them an exotic and expensive turkey for the big day.

'Quoth the Raven, "Nevermore."' Ravens have become synonymous with Edgar Allan Poe thanks to his poem about the bird, but did you know that the first bird mentioned in the Bible is a raven?

Thomas Bewick's *A History of British Birds* is said to have had a profound effect on the creative development of the Brontë sisters. In fact, this is the book that Jane Eyre is reading in the opening of Charlotte Brontë's famous novel.

Tudor cooks went to great lengths to impress their royal masters and mistresses. The 'four and twenty blackbirds baked in a pie' in the nursery rhyme is a reference to the spectacle where live blackbirds would be placed into a cooked pie crust and would fly out as the lid was lifted!

It seems that William Shakespeare was a bit of a birder – he mentions more than 50 species of birds across all his works.

What literary implement shares its name with a female swan? A pen, of course! A male swan is known as a cob.

THE MOST WONDERFUL TIME
OF THE YEAR

*Winter brings some amazing bird species
and spectacles to our shores.*

How many of these have you seen?

- Starling murmurations
- Waxwings feasting on berries
- Raptor roosts
- Common cranes
- Weird ducks
- High-tide wader spectacles
- Whooper and Bewick's swans
- City centre pied wagtail roosts (also seen in car parks and superstore roofs)
- Finch roosts.

FAVOURITE BIRD FACTS:
JAY

- The name 'Jay' sounds like the call, especially if you say it in an angry fashion, as the jay often does. The name has been in use since at least 1310.
- Jays can carry nine acorns at a time in their gullet – quite a heavy cargo!
- Despite their harsh alarm calls, jays also have a very quiet, musical, quite delightful bubbling song.

- Jays demonstrate a strange behaviour known as 'anting', which involves gathering insects in their bill and rubbing them over their plumage. This might help to rid them of feather parasites.
- In spring, when a female jay offers food to a male, the male takes it then offers it back. The female then seems to say, 'No, take it' and offers it back, and so on. 'No – you hang up!'
- On a single autumn day of collecting acorns, jays have been known to fly as far as 175km (109 miles) back and forth over multiple short trips.

BIZARRE BIRD NAMES

Some bird names make no sense at all!

The head of a black-headed gull is chocolate brown, not black – and that's only in the summer. And it's only a hood, not the whole head. In winter, this gull only has the odd smudge of black on its head.

The most obvious colour of a grey wagtail is a lovely citrine yellow, but there was already a yellow wagtail and a citrine wagtail, so this species was downgraded to grey. Unfortunately, there's further chance of name confusion, because the pied wagtail often looks rather – how shall I put it? – grey!

'Common' is a troubling, subjective epithet and it just doesn't work for the lovely common gull. It isn't rare, but in most parts of the country it is less common than other gulls.

The Iceland gull doesn't come from Iceland. (It's also never been seen scavenging outside the eponymous supermarket, to my knowledge.)

If the bearded tit was a tit (which it isn't) and had a beard (which it doesn't), the name would suit it perfectly.

CHRISTMAS CRACKERS

Birds' bills are surprisingly tough, and are specially adapted to perform a range of tasks. Let's see which bird can crack the toughest nut. . .

The hawfinch is famous for its ability to crack open the hardest of seeds. It does this using its huge bill, which is fitted with muscles so well developed that they make the cheeks bulge. The bill has two serrated knobs either side of the midline of both mandibles, which fit together and take the strain of splitting the seeds. Overall, the bill can put some 50kg (110lb) of pressure, crushing even the toughest seeds.

Hawfinches can crush olive seeds, as well as hornbeam. They can also bite through twigs to remove buds.

All finches also have a groove either side of the midline of the bill. They lodge seeds in the grooves and slit them open with the side of the mandible while rotating them with the tongue, like a tin opener.

Gulls often fly high and drop shellfish on to a hard surface, hoping to break them open. Although, sometimes they drop them on to sand, which softens the blow!

Woodpeckers, nuthatches, great tits and marsh tits often lodge nuts into crevices in order to hold them steady while they break into them by hammering at the end. Tits may hold seeds with their feet while they hammer at them.

The nutcracker of central Europe is a type of crow that hacks at pine seeds and hazel in a similar way. It has a specialised tongue to help de-husk them.

Carrion crows in Japan are remarkably intelligent. Walnut trees are often planted along roads and at intersections in cities like Tokyo and Kyoto. The crows have noticed that the tough fallen seeds are sometimes crushed by cars. Individuals have been seen taking the nuts, waiting for a red light at an intersection and then placing the nut in front of a car in order to crack it!

In South America, macaws are among the few birds that can open Brazil nuts.

The bone-eating lammergeier (a vulture found in mountains across Eurasia) is particularly partial to the marrow. Individuals will drop bones from a great height to dash them on rocks below.

Unfortunately for the reptiles, lammergeiers are also known to drop living tortoises from a height in order to smash their shells.

FAVOURITE BIRD FACTS:
JACKDAW

- Jackdaws are unusual among the bird fraternity because they have light grey eyes. The colour is not from pigment, but is the result of a rare arrangement of collagen fibres in the iris.
- These bright eyes are thought to act as signals in the dark, indicating to potential rivals that a nest hole is occupied.
- Jackdaws start incubation before the clutch is complete, meaning that some chicks hatch earlier than others. If food is in short supply, the younger chicks often starve thanks to their greedy siblings.

- Jackdaws sometimes rob puffins of their fish catch by ambushing them on the cliff-top, lying in wait in the grass!

SNOW WAS FALLING,
SNOW ON SNOW . . .

Four birds on the British List are named after snow: snow bunting, snow goose, snowy owl and snowy egret. The American snowy egret has only been recorded once.

Snow buntings breed further north than any other small bird in the world. They make cosy nests to stave off the cold, often lined with ptarmigan feathers.

The Snow Goose is a novella written in 1940 by the American author Paul Gallico. It's set in Essex, where snow geese don't occur as they are American birds.

Redpolls make tunnels in the snow to keep them warm at night. In one experiment in the Arctic, a redpoll burrow was found to be –14°C (6.8°F), while the outside temperature was –35°C (–31°F).

Snowy owls can survive the winter as far north as Ellesmere Island in Canada (82 degrees north), where it is dark all day and night in midwinter. They spend 92 per cent of their time just perching.

Green woodpeckers feed on ants throughout the winter. They have been known to dig through 30cm (12in) of snow to reach them on the ground.

Jays can also dig through snow to reach their stashed acorns, using visible landmarks to find them.

Goldcrests are so small that when snow covers the branches of conifer trees, the birds are light enough to edge among the needles in search of their favourite food – an obscure group of insect-like animals known as springtails.

Waxwings have been spotted trying to catch snowflakes in flight, in order to drink.

Wren mortality is highest in winter, because it takes the little birds huge amounts of energy to get through tough, snowy days.

Partridges apparently sometimes simply dive into soft snow from flight, and roost where they land!

The great grey owl of the northern hemisphere can hear the movement of rodents through the snow, and is able to reach them through 45cm (18in) of the white stuff.

Ptarmigans make burrows in the snow to keep warm. Snow can provide such good insulation that ptarmigans even seek out isolated snow patches in milder winters.

FAVOURITE BIRD FACTS:
RED-NECKED PHALAROPE

- Phalaropes are best-known for their buoyant swimming style, like cork-filled ducks, rather than wading.
- One of their main feeding methods is to spin round and round in the water in a tight circle, as if caught in a whirlpool. This spinning creates a vortex that lifts submerged prey to within reach.
- An individual phalarope always spins the same way. Some are clockwise spinners and others are anticlockwise spinners! They have been known to

spin at 54rpm, although they usually go slower than this.
- Red-necked phalaropes winter far out to sea, where they feed on plankton. Some individuals from Shetland winter off the coast of Peru. No one knows how they get there!
- Phalaropes also practise role reversal when breeding – the male is responsible for all incubation, brooding and care of the young.

IN THE DEEP MIDWINTER

*Winter is a challenging time for many species,
but some birds have adapted to survive in the
most amazing ways . . .*

Experiments have shown that snowy owls could survive temperatures down to –68°C (–90°F), although such temperates haven't been recorded in the Northern Hemisphere.

In winter, a blackbird can go without food for 2.2 days, or 4.6 days if it doesn't move about.

The survival of both treecreepers and sparrowhawks correlates to the amount of rainfall, rather than to snow or temperature. The more it rains, the lower their chances of making it through the winter.

Fish descend further in the sea in winter, so while guillemots typically dive down 20–50m (66–164ft) in summer, in winter they dive down 55–136m (180–446ft).

Ptarmigans survive in the far north where there are ten weeks of total darkness in winter. Air cavities in their feathers give them extra insulation.

Goldcrests slow down in very cold weather. At 15°C (59°F) they move at 8m (26ft) per minute, but at –18°C (–0.4°F) they move at 0.71m (2.3ft) per minute.

Have you ever seen a bird, such as a robin or a pigeon, look especially fat in the winter? The reason for that chubby appearance is that they increase the volume of insulating air between feather and skin, making the feathers stand more erect. This can increase insulation by a factor of three or more.

Birds save heat by a clever counter-current system. Where warm arterial blood enters exposed parts such as the legs, it flows alongside cold blood from veins that's on its way back to the heart. The heat from the arterial blood warms the blood in the veins, retaining heat inside the body.

Birds shiver to generate heat, just as we do.

Willow tits can reduce their body temperature from 38°C (100°F) to as low as 32°C (90°F) at night, in order to save energy.

Within the Arctic Circle, eiders spend 73 minutes a day feeding in the depths of winter.

BIRD NAMES THAT PEOPLE GET WRONG

We're all used to coming across the odd typo in print or on websites, but have you ever seen these embarrassing bird bloopers?

The white-fronted goose has become a Y-fronted goose (this has genuinely been quoted in the press)!

The mistle thrush has been unfortunately auto-corrected to missile thrush.

The whooper swan is often mentioned as the whopper swan. The whopper that whoops!

FAVOURITE BIRD FACTS:
CHAFFINCH

- The colourful, fresh-looking plumage of a spring chaffinch is actually not fresh at all. The feathers grow in autumn, and at that point the tips are dull. Wear and tear erodes the new, dull tips, unveiling the worn, colourful part of the feathers.
- A chaffinch's nest is one of the neatest and smartest made by any of our birds. It's exactly how you'd picture the perfect nest.

- Young chaffinches start singing in February, but at that time their song is not fully formed. They sound incomplete and often leave off the final flourish.
- Young chaffinches learn their songs from their father and neighbours.
- Vagrant chaffinches from Britain have reached North America.

A LONG TIME AGO . . .

*With the oldest bird fossils dating to around
150 million years ago, birds have a deep history,
a lot of which intertwines with our own.*

According to the Bible, Jesus mentioned birds a few times
during his ministry – most famously sparrows. In Matthew's
gospel (Chapter 10, verses 29–31) he says: 'Are not two
sparrows sold for a penny? Yet not one of them will fall to
the ground outside your Father's care. And even the very
hairs of your head are all numbered. So don't be afraid; you
are worth more than many sparrows.'

Dalmatian pelicans bred in the marshes around London,
but they were driven to extinction by the Romans about
2,000 years ago.

Hummingbirds once hovered around blooms in France.
Today, hummingbirds are only found in the Americas

(apart from a few vagrants in north-east Russia) but they are thought to have evolved in Europe. Fossils from 30–35 million years ago have been found in France, Germany and Poland.

In the past, swan meat was a delicacy for the uppermost classes, especially royalty. Henry III was a notable fan, who ordered 350 swans for the feast of Christmas in 1251.

A live dodo, brought from its home in Mauritius, was exhibited in London in 1638. The species became extinct sometime between 1662 and 1693 and we know almost nothing about it. In fact, we know more about the behaviour of many non-avian dinosaurs than we do about the dodo!

The first escaped ring-necked parakeets to nest in Britain were recorded in – can you guess? Bet you can't! 1855.

Black grouse bred in southern England, in Kent, Berkshire, Surrey, Hampshire, Dorset and Devon, until the beginning of the 20th century.

House sparrows are almost certainly the only birds in the world that have coevolved with people, as they are largely dependent upon us for their survival. They are thought to have evolved 10,000 years ago, with the rise of agriculture.

AWKWARD RELATIVES

At Christmas, we often have to put up with relatives who, shall we say, test our patience a little! But that's nothing compared to the awkward associations thrown up by recent DNA studies of bird families.

The closest relative of the bearded tit is . . . the skylark (and other larks). See the family connection? No, I can't either!

Grebes are obviously not remotely related to flamingos. Or are they? Turns out that the pink waders are the grebe's nearest relations. Well, they both have feathers and like water . . .

Falcons are birds of prey, but it seems that they aren't as closely related to other birds of prey such as eagles, hawks or buzzards. Instead, by far the closest relatives of peregrines, kestrels and merlins are . . . parrots!

FAVOURITE BIRD FACTS:
RED KITE

- Red kites were common scavengers in London in the Middle Ages. Shakespeare called the capital 'The City of Kites and Crows'.
- These medieval kites had a reputation for snatching laundry from washing lines in order to add material to their nest.
- Although best known for eating dead meat, red kites can be predatory, especially when breeding. They will snatch up rabbits, rats, voles and even other birds, notably young crows and gulls.

MISTLETOE AND WINE

*Mistletoe is a familiar sight at Christmas,
but how much do you know about this iconic plant?*

Mistletoe grows in bunches on trees, and is partly parasitic.
It gets most of its nutrients and water from the tree on which
it grows, but it can also photosynthesise itself. It produces
tiny, insect-pollinated flowers between February and April.

Mistletoe is almost unique among British plants in
producing white berries, so many birds never learn to eat it.

The mistle thrush is one of the few birds that does enjoy
feasting on the nutritious berries. Its English name and its
scientific name – *viscivorus* (mistletoe-eater) – reflect this.

Species such as redwings, fieldfares and blackbirds are often
attracted by the sight of the mistle thrushes eating the
berries, so the thrushes often spend much of the winter

defending their personal supply of mistletoe berries against other birds. If all goes well, the requisitioned clumps will nourish them until early spring.

Among common British birds, blackcaps are also partial to the berries but the rarer waxwing also eats them.

There are lots of mistletoe species in the world and many birds eat them. In Australia, there is even a mistletoebird and in South America there is a mistletoe tyrannulet.

Mistletoe berries are very sticky inside. Indeed, the pulp was once used as a birdlime, to ensnare the feet of birds for eating.

Birds don't drink wine, but they sometimes do get drunk! The main cause is fermented berries. There are records of waxwings (especially the American cedar waxwing) becoming completely intoxicated and unable to fly in a straight line! Cedar waxwings have even been known to die of alcohol poisoning, their livers destroyed.

The small tropical bird the bananaquit is especially partial to alcoholic drinks. In the Caribbean, it apparently prefers drinks of 4–6 per cent proof – any more is too much!

WE THREE KINGS (AND MORE)

Technically, every unmarked mute swan in open water belongs to the monarch.

Canada geese first appeared in Britain during the time of Charles II, who added them to his wildfowl collection in St James's Park around 1670. They can still be seen in the park today, along with pelicans.

There are many birds worldwide named after kings. Those on the British List include, of course, the common kingfisher (and the vagrant Belted kingfisher), plus a rare duck known as the king eider and America's eastern kingbird.

Goldcrests and firecrests belong to a family collectively known as kinglets (*Regulidae*). They're named after the colourful 'crown' on their heads.

The emperor penguin is the largest and most powerful, trumping the king penguin.

Not a single bird in the world includes the word 'queen'.

King Cnut (Canute) ruled England, Denmark and Norway ('Me three kings'?). The legend that he claimed he could hold the tide back is not likely to be true – kinder versions suggest that he was simply demonstrating his lack of omnipotence. But I digress. The scientific name of the spectacular shorebird the knot (*Calidris canutus*) derives from King Cnut. The bird itself, of course, famously rides the tides. The English name, knot, possibly derives from its unremarkable call.

FAVOURITE BIRD FACTS: SKYLARK

- Skylarks are around us all year long, not just in summer. If you listen carefully, you may well hear a skylark singing in winter.
- The skylark's song is one of the longest of any bird. The average is 2.2 minutes, but they have been known to sing continuously for 20 minutes!
- Their song is unusual in being a continuous stream of notes, rather than the more common collection of clear phrases.
- All a skylark does in flight is undulate slightly up and down. The lack of aerobatics is probably an adaptation for prolonged singing, which they even do when being chased by a predator.

THE HOLLY AND THE IVY

*There is no doubt that these two evergreens
provide more than their fair share of Christmas
cheer — not just to us, but to birds too.*

Holly berries mature in late September and may still be available the following July, making them the longest-lasting berries. They don't drop from the tree or go bad, and they aren't damaged by cold. Only the female tree produces them.

Almost every berry-eating bird eats holly berries, including all the thrushes.

Mistle thrushes will defend individual holly trees or clumps for the whole winter, in the same way that they defend mistletoe. They use holly as a personal food source, mainly for emergencies.

The average holly leaf lasts for seven years and the tree's dense foliage is ideal for nesting and roosting birds. Large clumps of ivy are also great for nesting.

Ivy is the only berry-bearing plant that flowers in the autumn, when insects such as bees, wasps and red admiral butterflies swarm to its blooms.

Ivy berries are available during birds' 'hunger gap' (February to April) when other berries are becoming scarce. It's a godsend to many birds, so don't cut it down!

Many birds nest in ivy, including treecreepers and spotted flycatchers.

THE CLASSICAL CHRISTMAS

Between 1784 and 1787, Mozart had a pet starling, which learnt to whistle the opening bars of his Piano Concerto No. 17. When the bird died, the composer arranged an elaborate funeral for it, writing a poem and getting attendees to sing at the ceremony.

In Germany, it was once common for people to teach captive bullfinches to sing. Apparently, the birds could whistle the German national anthem well!

Beethoven was keen on birds, and incorporated their songs into some of his works. Most notable is the second movement of his Symphony No. 6 (the Pastoral). At the end of the movement, you can hear representations of nightingale, quail and cuckoo. All three of these tend to sing in the half-light and all were common near Vienna in summer in the early 1800s. By the time Beethoven wrote this piece, encroaching deafness meant he could hardly hear birdsong any more.

The 'Spring' movement of Vivaldi's *Four Seasons* contains violin trills and flourishes that represent birdsong.

A piece by Finnish composer Einojuhani Rautavaara called *Cantus Arcticus* (1972) includes recordings of real birdsong.

Grieg's Piano Concerto opens with a famously explosive flourish that is notably similar in structure and verve to the song of the Cetti's warbler (have a listen and see what you think). However, Grieg wrote the concerto in Denmark, where there were no Cetti's warblers at the time.

FAVOURITE BIRD FACTS:
SONG THRUSH

- Unusually, song thrushes have no obvious visual courtship display – they just get on with things!
- Male song thrushes stop singing as soon as they are paired, although they can still be heard as part of the dawn chorus.
- A study revealed that the song thrush's favourite foods were earthworms (March to April), snails (June to July) and spiders (late summer).
- Song thrushes all have their favourite 'anvils' – hard surfaces on which they smash snails and even cherries.

FACTS ABOUT TURKEYS

Turkey is the traditional dish at Christmas, but how much do you really know about these funny-looking birds?

The wild turkey is the only bird from the Americas to have been domesticated worldwide.

The name 'turkey' used to refer to domestic guinea fowl.

The name given to the bird has nothing to do with the country now called the Republic of Türkiye ('land of the Turks'). However, it is rather wonderful that the Turkish name for the turkey is *hindi*, meaning 'India'.

Some people maintain that turkeys are so stupid that they may drown themselves by looking up into the rain!

American founding father Benjamin Franklin wanted the turkey to be the emblem of the United States rather than the bald eagle.

Early settlers to the Americas brought domestic turkeys with them – a classic case of bringing coals to Newcastle!

Male turkeys give their famous gobbling calls from a perch in a tree.

Despite their size, turkeys are highly elusive in the wild.

THAT'S A FACT – OR IS IT?

Ever wondered if those popular facts about birds are true?
Allow me to clear some of them up for you.

A MUTE SWAN CAN BREAK YOUR ARM

This is complete codswallop. However, there was a case where someone was accidentally drowned by an angry mute swan after their canoe overturned.

MAGPIES STEAL WEDDING RINGS

Despite the popular myth – and Rossini's opera *The Thieving Magpie* – this isn't true at all. Theft of shiny objects is much more typical of the magpie's relative, the jackdaw.

BIRDS SING FOR JOY

Sorry, but this isn't true either. Birds sing to proclaim territory and to attract a mate. Most female birds don't sing at all in Britain and Europe. Are only the males allowed to be 'joyful'?

WOODPECKERS MAKE THEIR DRUMMING SOUND WHEN EXCAVATING HOLES

No. The drumming sound really is drumming – hitting the wood in order to make a resonant noise. When making holes, the bird doesn't hit the wood as quickly or as evenly.

FAVOURITE BIRD FACTS:
STARLING

- A starling flies at 60–80km/h (37–50mph).
- Starlings have an unusual feeding method called 'prying'. They insert their bill into the ground, then use its incredibly strong muscles to open it, making a hole. They then peer in, hoping to find something edible. Starlings also use their sense of smell to find food in the soil.
- In 1890–91, 100 individual starlings were introduced to Central Park, New York. The North American population now totals 200 million pairs – a successful conquest!
- A starling sings throughout the year and its song improves throughout its life. The larger the starling colony, the wider the birds' repertoire.

- Male starlings bring aromatic plants such as yarrow into their nests, possibly to impress females or to enhance the health of the chicks.

STARS (THE HEAVENS)

Just like human navigators, some birds depend on the stars in our sky to help them on their journeys.

The starling is named for the white dots on its plumage, which were somewhat fancifully thought to look like stars.

During migration, many species of birds orientate themselves using the stars, as the Wise Men did.

Birds tend to perceive the rotation of the firmament around the North Star, rather than the details of individual stars.

Delightful experiments in the USA have revealed that young indigo buntings learn the arrangement of the firmament at night while in the nest.

The Sun is a star, of course, and birds also use it to navigate. They have such an accurate internal clock that they can adjust for the Sun's perceived movements across the sky.

Many of a bird's natural rhythms are determined by day-length – the amount of sunlight there is.

There is a hummingbird called a shining sunbeam.

FAVOURITE BIRD FACTS: LONG-TAILED TIT

- Long-tailed tits live in family groups for most of the year. Young birds remain with adults into the winter, and first-year females leave to join neighbouring flocks in early spring.
- It's common for relatives to help out with feeding young long-tailed tits. Up to eight helpers may be hanging around.
- The remarkable nests contain four ingredients: moss (main bulk), cobwebs (binding), lichen (camouflage) and feathers (interior decoration).
- Both sexes build the nest. This may take up to 33 days, but the tits only work in the mornings! Their homes are usually built low down, but occasionally you can see a long-tailed tit's nest in the fork of a tree, up to 35m (115ft) above the ground!
- Long-tailed tits eat tiny morsels of food, even the eggs of moths and butterflies.

SILENT NIGHT

The nights are long at this time of year.
What happens in bird world after dark?

When it's very cold, wrens may roost together in bodily contact. Normally they prefer to roost alone.

Skylarks roost on the ground, out in the open in fields. They usually select a slight hollow – but it must be cold!

Partridges also roost on the ground, sometimes in tight groups with bodily contact to keep them toasty.

Long-tailed tits are famous for cuddling up together at night. Family units, including the previous year's youngsters, huddle together to survive cold temperatures. But it's a system based on seniority – the adults ensure they're in the middle, while the younger birds occupy the outer perches!

Gadwalls spend 50 per cent of even daylight hours asleep. They open one eye every few minutes, and one of the brain's hemispheres always stays awake. This is described as 'quiet sleep and relaxed wakefulness' which sounds heavenly!

Swifts famously sleep on the wing, taking short naps and also keeping one hemisphere of the brain constantly active.

Resident chaffinches that breed in Britain remain in their territories and roost alone. Continental winter visiting chaffinches roost in large groups with other finches.

Blue tits and great tits roost in cavities such as tree holes. They probably sleep throughout the hours of darkness.

Gulls roost on the water, either at sea or on large inland waters such as reservoirs. They often commute between the sea and fields each winter day.

FAVOURITE BIRD FACTS:
GOLDCREST

- Despite their tiny size, goldcrests regularly migrate across the North Sea in a single flight, from Norway to Britain.
- Goldcrests may die if they get stuck in a spider's web.
- The song of the male goldcrest ends with a flourish. Each male has up to 28 different endings in its repertoire.
- Goldcrests often hover at the end of branches to pick at insects that are hard to reach.

CHRISTMAS TREES
(AND OTHER PLANTS)

Commercial Christmas trees tend to be Norway spruce and Nordmann (Caucasian) firs. Neither of these are native to Britain, although they are widely planted. Let's take a look at some birds' associations with particular trees.

The siskin breeds in Norway spruce, but in autumn it switches to birch trees, and then to alders in late winter.

Redpolls are associated with birch trees all year round, nesting in their branches. A redpoll's winter diet may reach 90 per cent birch seeds.

Three breeding species are characteristic of woods of sessile oak in the west and north of Britain – pied flycatcher, redstart and wood warbler.

The hawfinch is strongly associated with hornbeam.

Waxwings depend heavily on rowan trees in the autumn and winter. It is when rowan crops fail in Russia or the region known as Fennoscandia that waxwings appear in larger numbers in Britain.

Bramblings are strongly associated with beech in the winter. In fact, their lovely orange colour has evolved to resemble the colour of autumn beech leaves.

On the continent, short-toed treecreepers struggle with the smooth trunks of beech trees because of their short toes! British treecreepers fare much better!

FAVOURITE BIRD FACTS: GOLDEN EAGLE

- Evidence suggests that golden eagles may be almost as fast through the air as peregrines. Speeds of 240–320km/h (150–200mph) have been claimed, as well as 50km/h (31mph) in level flight.
- The nest of a golden eagle can be huge, as refurbishments may go on for years. Some have been discovered that are 7m (23ft) tall, and others have been found that are made partly of deer antlers.

- Most eagles lay two eggs, several days apart. They start incubation with the first, which means that one hatches several days later and the younger eagle chick is often killed by the older.
- Golden eagles occasionally kill larger animals such as young deer by gripping the neck and 'riding' on the wounded animal until it perishes.

DECK THE HALLS!

We're not the only species to decorate our homes. Birds also adorn their nests — although not especially for Christmas!

Female blue tits bring aromatic plants such as mint and lavender into their nests. No one knows for sure why they do this, but these plants are thought to kill bacteria.

Male wrens often build several nests in their territory, which they present to females, who choose which one they prefer. However, these 'cock-nests' are only the outer part, and the female takes over lining and decorating the interior!

Whitethroats and other related warblers also build cock-nests. The females may choose to build an entirely separate nest, though!

Nuthatches collect large amounts of mud, and plaster it around the entrance to their nesting hole to keep out competitors. They also insist on spreading flakes of bark to help line the nest. They prefer to get this flooring from pine trees which, for a bird that lives in deciduous woods, can be hard to find!

The black wheatear of Spain, Portugal and North Africa collects hundreds of stones to build a rampart in front of its nest, or to pile them up nearby. Both sexes collect stones, but nobody knows why.

Australasian bowerbirds collect large numbers of artefacts – often blue ones – to decorate their bower. These seem to serve no function other than to impress a mate.

CHRISTMAS STOCKINGS

Okay, it's not quite the same meaning as what we leave out for Santa to fill with presents, but several species of birds stock up on food to get them through the winter.

Coal tits can often be seen approaching bird feeders and then darting away as soon as they've procured an item. They will often store seeds and other foodstuffs away to eat later.

Willow tits store lots of items, including seeds and insects, around their territory – for example, in loose bark or clumps of lichen. In some parts of the world, these birds might store an estimated 460,000 items a year!

Jays collect up to 5,000 acorns in the autumn and hide them all away, each in a different place – this is known as scatter-hoarding. Many aren't eaten and grow into oak trees, which benefits other jays in the future.

Many species of owls cache food in the winter, especially in very cold climates. For example, they may store small mammals in tree holes. When hungry, they sit on frozen prey to thaw them out!

Great grey shrikes also set up larders, often impaling their prey on thorns or barbed wire. They do this at any time of year. Male shrikes sometimes select the very best cached food to feed to females to whom they are not paired!

FAVOURITE BIRD FACTS:
BEARDED TIT

- This wonderful bird might justifiably be called the 'most unique' of all Britain's bird species, as it's the only member of its family (*Panuridae*). The only other bird on the British List in its own family, the wallcreeper (*Tichodromidae*), is a rare visitor.
- It is also one of Britain's most specialised birds in terms of habitat, living only among reed beds. When population levels are high, individuals 'erupt' from a reed bed and travel away looking for pastures new.

- In autumn, bearded tits switch diet from insects to seeds. To cope with this, their stomach develops hard plates and they swallow hundreds of small stones to aid digestion.
- Copulation for bearded tits lasts 15 seconds.
- Pairs of bearded tits get through broods quickly and can theoretically raise 10–20 young in a season. Juveniles brought up early in the season may sometimes breed themselves in August of the same year.
- Bearded tits have an exciting autumn display known as 'high flying', in which birds lift 50–60m (164–197ft) into the sky, calling loudly.

LET'S PARTY!

*Whether you're a party animal or a confirmed introvert,
there's no escape from socialising at Christmas. But what
about birds — do they always flock together?*

Pied wagtails don't conform to a type. In winter, they either
move around as part of a flock, or they hold a territory,
depending on the individual.

Many species, including blue tits and yellowhammers, are
resolutely territorial in spring, but sociable in winter.

Marsh tits remain as pairs in their own territory all year
round. They might join roaming flocks, but only within the
borders of their territory.

Robins are the scrooges of Christmas – usually quite happy
to be left alone!

Bramblings take their social skills too far, gathering in sometimes enormous roosting parties. The largest ever congregation was estimated at 12 million!

Blackbirds are like the rude uncle that nobody wants to invite at Christmas. They're largely loners, but they roost together and make a lot of aggressive 'chinking' calls in the evening, complaining about life, no doubt!

Choughs are the ultimate chillaxers. They live in pairs, but gather in flocks readily. Everyone's invited, nobody is pressured into staying longer than they want, and all are welcome back any time.

Bird-flock shenanigans occur just as frequently as when humans get together. Species from ducks to yellowhammers to siskins meet potential partners in winter flocks.

BIRDS NAMED AFTER CHRISTMAS

Six birds have 'Christmas' in their name. But truth be told, they're all named after two Christmas Islands!

The Christmas Island that lies south of Java has five native birds named after it, including the Christmas Island frigatebird. (This is the Christmas Island famous for its red crabs.)

The other Christmas Island is near Hawaii. The Christmas shearwater (*Puffinus nativitatis*) is named after it.

Of course, there are lots of birds named after Santa (that is, saints), including the St Helena plover, Santa Cruz ground dove and the Santa Marta wren.

FAVOURITE BIRD FACTS: HOUSE SPARROW

- House sparrows usually pair up in autumn rather than spring.
- The amount of black on a male house sparrow's chin/breast is directly related to its fighting ability and, presumably, its testosterone levels.
- Some males deliberately dust-bathe to wipe the pale tips off their feathers in order to show more black.
- House sparrows live in permanent colonies, often occupying the same neighbourhood for life.
- They remain in their territory all year round, except briefly in late summer, when they go on a little holiday!

LITTLE DRUMMER BOYS
(AND GIRLS)

'Come, they told me pa rum pum pum pum . . .'.
If you listen hard enough on a walk through the woods,
you may be lucky enough hear our very own drummers,
tapping out a tune on the tree trunks.

The great spotted woodpecker has various adaptations, including a thickened skull, to ensure that it doesn't do itself any damage while excavating. Its tongue is so long that the bird has to wrap it around the back of its skull when it's not in use!

Great spotted woodpeckers can identify creatures lurking behind the bark of a tree simply by tapping – a bit like knocking on a wall to find a secret passageway.

Both sexes of woodpeckers drum and both excavate burrows. Copulation is poorly studied in woodpeckers, but it must sometimes be impaired owing to one or both birds having a headache!

When drumming, the great spotted woodpecker beats its bill against wood 15–20 times a second.

The green woodpecker is very unusual in having a highly specialised diet – it feeds almost exclusively on ants. These insects can comprise well over 80 per cent of the green woodpecker's annual diet.

The green woodpecker's tongue sticks out 10cm (4in) beyond its bill. It also has huge salivary glands to help lick up its favourite ant food.

Green woodpeckers sometimes roost down rabbit burrows.

Lesser spotted woodpeckers quite often hammer at reed stems in marshes.

In Sweden, 10 per cent of female lesser spotted woodpeckers have two mates.

FAVOURITE BIRD FACTS:
DIPPER

- The dipper is the only aquatic songbird (although there are four other species of dipper in other parts of the world).
- The dipper's three favourite foods are mayfly nymphs, caddisfly nymphs and stonefly nymphs – in that order.
- Dippers have incredibly dense down under their feathers, and twice as many feathers as non-aquatic songbirds of the same size. These help them to survive winter temperatures of −45°C (−49°F) and even allow the birds to feed under the ice.

- Dippers get their name from their habit of 'dipping' up and down. No one has worked out why they do this, but it may be a signal to other birds.
- Their eyelids are white!

GHOSTS OF CHRISTMAS . . .

PAST

The great auk is the only recent (that is, not simply a fossil) bird on the British List that is officially extinct. It is also the only flightless one. The eskimo curlew is almost certainly extinct, too, but remains officially classed (2025) as Critically Endangered.

In a glorious, if tragic, case of muddied waters, the all-but-extinct slender-billed curlew was recorded in Northumberland in May 1998, but then the record was rejected. It was then accepted again – and then rejected! The bird was last recorded in Hungary in 2001.

PRESENT

Other than the eskimo curlew (see above), the Balearic shearwater is the only bird on the British List that is officially classed as Critically Endangered.

Nobody knows their own future, let alone that of birds, but in 40 years' time, when you are reading a battered copy of this book from a charity shop, some British birds might have disappeared. The turtle dove is a candidate for extinction, and things look pretty worrying for British populations of willow tit, wood warbler and lesser spotted woodpecker.

WILLOWS TO MAKE YOU WEEP

In the whole world of birds, only four species have the epithet 'willow'. And all four of them are part of a species pair that birdwatchers find difficult to tell apart.

The willow warbler is difficult to distinguish from a chiffchaff. It has longer wings, a flatter crown and yellower plumage, but most of the time people just merge the names and refer to them as willowchiffs.

A willow tit is so hard to tell from marsh tit that until 1897, nobody realised that it occurred in Britain. Even then, it took two German ornithologists examining a tray of 'marsh tit' skins in the British Museum to realise that they weren't what they seemed. One of the discoverers, Otto Kleinschmidt, had the scientific name of the newly described subspecies (*Poecile montanus kleinschmidti*), named after him. The bird was the last widespread British species to be added to the British List, in 1900.

The willow grouse, also known as the willow ptarmigan, is the continental version of the red grouse. It is very hard to distinguish from the rock ptarmigan, although it has a heavier bill.

The willow flycatcher is an American species, and it was only in 1973 that it was separated from the almost identical alder flycatcher. The latter has been recorded in Britain, but only from DNA analysis of some poo on a rock. There's no point trying to identify them from the trees they're found in either, because their breeding habitats often overlap. A willow flycatcher may perch in an alder and vice versa. Their calls might be more helpful – the willow flycatcher calls 'fitz-bew' and the alder flycatcher 'fee-BEE-o'.

FAVOURITE BIRD FACTS: HONEY-BUZZARD

- This large, strange bird of prey has fantastic flying skills, specialising in pursuing wasps and their grubs.
- It spends hours watching the comings and goings of these insects, eventually following them to their nest. They have been seen snatching wasps from the eaves of houses and may dig in the ground up to 40cm (16in) to reach a nest.
- It has been known to walk continuously for 500m (1,640ft) on the ground while foraging.

- The bird probably looks like a buzzard in a rare avian example of Batesian mimicry – that is, it looks like something scary and powerful to ward off trouble from goshawks.
- In one particularly strange performance, a honey-buzzard was seen plucking branches off maple and oak trees and laying them in a pile on the ground. It then sat on the pile and stretched out its wings to their fullest extent. The leaves may have been laid out to attract ants, which would then crawl over the honey-buzzard's plumage, where their excretions may provide chemical protection.

UNUSUAL MIGRATIONS

*A lot of bird species make long, challenging journeys every year
to travel to their breeding and wintering grounds. But some of
these long-haul flights are more surprising than others . . .*

Two flycatchers, two very different autumn migrations . . .
Pied flycatchers from western Europe all fly to northern
Portugal and Spain, where they fatten up for a long flight.
Some or all go on to do the same in North Africa. Then they
all overfly the Sahara in one long flight lasting 40–60 hours
until they reach West Africa. Spotted flycatchers have a
similar destination, but make their journey gradually, with
lots of short hops that are often dictated by rains. Spotted
flycatchers usually stop for a few days in Saharan oases.

After breeding, most of Europe's shelduck population
gathers off the Dutch/German coast for the summer. They
leave their young behind and the adults congregate on
the vast mudflats of the Wadden Sea, where there is lots

of food and excellent socialising. Summer, crowds, noise, mud . . . remind you of anything? It's basically the shelduck's Glastonbury.

Water pipits breed in the upland meadows of central Europe, 1,400–2,500m (4,600–8,200ft) above sea level. In the autumn, however, they are drawn to the damp lowland meadows and watercress beds of Britain. To get here, they have to fly north in autumn, which is, of course, the 'wrong' direction.

Quail migrations have been famous for centuries, and are even mentioned in the Bible! In recent years, it's become clear just how extraordinary quail movement is. They migrate from North America in spring, and breed in southern Europe. They then migrate north in July, and breed again – often in Britain. Some of these midsummer breeders may be young that hatched earlier in the year.

In crossbreeding experiments, scientists found that if you pair a blackcap from a migrant population (from Sweden, for example) with a bird from a resident population (such as Madeira), the offspring showed migratory tendencies intermediate between the two. From this, we can deduce that migratory paths are inherited.

The lesser black-backed gull is a candidate for undertaking the most leisurely migration of any bird. After leaving breeding areas in the Netherlands in the autumn and travelling an average 1,200km (7,456 miles), these birds only moved around 44km (27 miles) a day. It would almost be quicker to walk!

FAVOURITE BIRD FACTS:
RUFF

- This amazing wader has a complicated courtship system. In the spring, male ruffs perform a communal display at a gathering known as a lek. The 10–12 males on the lek fight there. Amazingly, all the displays occur in complete silence.
- The top birds own the best territories on the lek, often slightly elevated, so the females can recognise the best males. They mate there, but the sexes form no relationship beyond the act of copulation.

- Some males travel from lek to lek, without holding a territory. They specialise in mating with females who are queuing for the top male! These males are known as satellite ruffs and have white plumage (not whiter than white, though!).
- The ruff is the world's most naturally variable bird, with around 800 different plumage types.
- The variable colours of the males may be adapted to signal individual identity in the absence of a song or song-flight.

FASCINATING BEHAVIOUR

*How many of these brilliant British bird
behaviours have you witnessed?*

STARLING MURMURATIONS
- Starling murmurations are usually spotted at dusk, but they also take place at dawn. This dawn departure is a sight to behold, as the birds don't all go off at once but at staggered three-minute intervals.
- Starling murmurations can be among the largest bird gatherings on Earth.
- In Britain, they are at their best between November and January.
- Many of the birds taking part are migrants to Britain, often from eastern Europe. They may come to join the roost from as much as 50km (31 miles) away.

- The starlings fly in without calling. Only the whirring of the wings is heard until the birds have settled.
- In the aerobatic display, each bird manages to avoid the others by taking note of the positions of their seven nearest neighbours.
- The precise function of all the aerobatics is not fully understood, but it is probably an invitation for others to come and join the multitude.
- There are potential advantages to mass roosting. The more birds there are, the less chance there is of any one individual being preyed on.
- Once settled, the birds may keep close enough to benefit from body heat. They are thought to monitor the health of their roost-mates, and may benefit from determining who looks well fed, and following them to profitable feeding grounds the next day.

DAWN CHORUS

- The dawn chorus actually takes place in the darkness before sunrise – before the dawn. Conditions at this time are often calm and there is little ambient noise, which makes it a good time to sing. Birdsong carries 20 times further at dawn than it does at midday.

- It lasts about 20 minutes on average.
- Different species sing at different times. Robins are often first to start up, because they have comparatively large eyes that are used to low light conditions. Great tits, blue tits and chiffchaffs are fairly late risers!
- In Britain, the singers in the dawn chorus are mostly males. Females apparently sleep through some of it!
- The reason behind the swell of singing before dawn isn't fully understood. It may be a kind of roll-call for everyone to declare that they are still alive and on territory.

V FORMATION

- Birds in a V formation have a 'leader', but always only a temporary one. Birds at the front work harder, so the positions change regularly. (Nobody knows how they work it out.)
- It is mainly large birds that make these formations: ducks, geese, swans, ibises, cranes, gulls, pelicans and waders. When a large bird is flying, the tips of the wings create a vortex of rotating air. Immediately behind the air is pushed down, but off to the side there is an equal updraft, and it is

this that the following bird 'rides'. For smaller birds, the energy-saving gains aren't enough.

- In case it ever comes in handy, the ideal position (in pelican flocks, at least) is about 1m (3.3ft) behind and 1m to the side of the wingtip in front!
- A bird on its own has a faster heart rate and flaps more than the equivalent species in a flock.
- Young birds aren't as good at flying in the perfect V. It's a skill that has to be learned.

FAVOURITE BIRD FACTS: NIGHTJAR

- Nightjars are nocturnal, and feed on insects that fly at dusk and at night, such as moths and beetles. They also drink in flight, the same way a swallow does.
- They are the only British birds that often breed according to the phases of the Moon.
- They try to coordinate feeding of their young around the full moon, when insects are easier to catch.
- They have tactile bristles around their mouth, which helps them to grip their prey.

GREAT BRITISH MIMICS

Everybody knows that starlings are excellent at imitating the sounds of other birds, but they're not the only birds with a talent for mimicry.

The starling is not the best mimic in Britain by any measure, having only about 20 copied sounds of other birds in its repertoire.

The marsh warbler is the very best – known to copy about 200 species. Amazingly, a young bird learns half its imitations in Europe and half in its African winter quarters. Its whole song is mimetic.

Many warblers include mimicry in their songs, including sedge warblers, reed warblers and common whitethroats.

Robins imitate lots of species, especially blue tits.

Jays often mimic buzzards and tawny owls.

Some lesser-known songbirds, such as whinchats, wheatears and redstarts, also include mimicry.

Blackbirds do imitate other birds, but they are more celebrated for imitating human-made sounds such as whistles, car alarms and so on.

SANTA'S REINDEER
ARE . . . BIRDS

The first mention of reindeer pulling Santa's sleigh was in a poem of 1821. But of course, birds fly much more quickly and skilfully than grazing mammals with four legs and no wings, so if Santa's reindeer were birds, what species would they be?

Dasher: Lots of birds dash, but not many dash with the same panache as a kingfisher – which could also be the royal sleigh-puller!

Dancer: No birds dance on the ground quite like cranes, but the ultimate 'sky-dancer' is surely the hen harrier, whose display is a joyful exercise in aerobatic abandon. It might send the sleigh spinning out of control, though.

Prancer: To prance means to move with high springy steps, so perhaps its bird form would be a bittern moving in a reed bed, or maybe a water rail. Both species are used to flying at night, which will be helpful.

Vixen: This one's a little tricky and we're going to have to go abroad, to either the USA, where we can find a fox sparrow, or to Africa, where there's a bird called a foxy cisticola.

Comet: Again, it has to be an exotic species. Several hummingbirds are known as comets, and they're all as gorgeous as they sound. Pulling a sleigh will be hard work for such a small bird, but it's Christmas, so magic abounds.

Cupid: The garden robin often pairs up at Christmas, so what better bird to have for such an important task? If any robins are unavailable owing to Christmas card modelling commitments, there is a group of parrots known as lovebirds that could fill in.

Donner: It's appropriate to choose an Australian bird here – because this is one of the first places Santa visits on his journey round the earth. The golden whistler is a great songster, and is often stimulated to sing by loud noises, including the thunderclaps from which this reindeer gets its name.

Blitzen: It's a long journey going around the globe, so the swift, with its lightning-fast bursts of speed, is a good one to add to the team. It's also used to high altitudes.

Rudolph: Well, nothing does a red nose better than a puffin! Strictly speaking it's the beak not the nose, but careful readers might have noticed that the science hasn't got in the way of this section!

FAVOURITE BIRD FACTS:
BLACK-NECKED GREBE

- In autumn, the entire US population of black-necked grebes gathers on two salt lakes – Lake Mono, California, and Great Salt Lake, Utah – to moult and feast on brine shrimps and alkali flies.
- There, they allow their wing muscles to shrivel while the digestive organs vastly increase in size. These changes in proportions are the largest recorded for any bird in the world.
- The black-necked grebe is flightless for longer than any flying bird in the world – up to eight months.
- It then flies to its winter quarters on sheltered coasts in December to January, later than any other bird.

AMAZING BRITISH BIRD SOUNDS

*Try to hear these bird sounds — in the wild or on
an app — and see if you agree with my descriptions.*

The siskin has a rambling, lively song typical of finches.
However, every so often it intersperses its rambles with a
delightful – and quite hilarious – extended buzz, sounding
like a mechanical toy.

Golden plover – oh my goodness, that song! Needle-sharp,
clear, deeply melancholic . . .

The jack snipe doesn't breed in Britain, but in its home in
the far north of Europe, it makes a sound like a distant piece
of machinery, or maybe cantering horses.

The word 'tittering' might have been invented for the sound
that comes out of the little grebe.

The lovely, shivering main song of a wood warbler has a
silvery trill, like a spinning coin coming to rest.

The capercaillie makes an incredible sound – something like a bouncing ball followed by a champagne cork popping!

The nightjar sounds like a two-stroke motorcycle engine. It's a sort of long, wooden-sounding trill on two notes.

Some consider the woodlark's song the loveliest of all British bird songs. It's a gorgeous lilting, gentle phrase that steps down the scale in semitones.

At the display ground, male black grouse give a delicious dove-like cooing interspersed by guttural sounds. It's been brilliantly described as the background sound of hot springs, with simmering and the occasional explosion of gas.

The shoveler's display calls faintly recall the steady beats of an old-fashioned typewriter.

Puffins sound like somebody who is very drunk and very tired, laughing at a joke they don't understand.

A woodcock sounds like a frog croaking before being rapidly stepped on!

The sound of the eider might recall some women in their golden years reacting to the unveiling of a nude sculpture.

FAVOURITE BIRD FACTS:
PUFFIN

- Puffins often live into their twenties or even thirties. Equivalent land birds rarely reach double figures in Britain.
- Being long-lived and faithful to their colonies, puffins have to breed next to the same neighbours year after year!
- Puffins have two brood patches, but only lay one egg. In the distant past, their ancestors must have laid two eggs.

- Puffins carry fish in their bill, held in place partly by backward-pointing projections from the sides, and by the tongue. They normally bring half a dozen fish at a time, but a puffin was once recorded carrying 62 fish!

WEIRD AND WONDERFUL WADERS

*Waders are a diverse group of birds that can be found all over
the world. As their name suggests, they typical live in wet,
coastal environments and have long legs which allow them
to wade up and down the shoreline in the hunt for food.
Look out for a wading species next time you're at the beach.*

Almost every wader nests on the ground, but the green
sandpiper lays its eggs in the old nests of other birds, such as
fieldfares or pigeons, in bushes well above ground.

If a green sandpiper fails to breed in Scandinavia, it may cut
its losses and fly south to the UK to enjoy a summer of
relaxation. After all, there's always next season.

Sanderlings are famous for scurrying along beaches while
dodging the waves. They need to be very good runners, so
evolution has dispensed with their hind toe. They only have
three toes, all pointing forward.

Which bird grows the brightest white feathers? The super-camouflaged woodcock doesn't seem a likely winner here, but in tests, the underside of its tail feathers outshines the plumage of every other white bird. The feathers are usually covered, but are visible during the woodcock's twilight display.

The first full moon in November is traditionally called the 'woodcock moon', as it often coincides with an arrival of the birds into the UK.

The curlew's and whimbrel's generic scientific name is *Numenius*, which is Greek for 'new moon', after the crescent-like curve of the bill.

Coincidentally, the whimbrel's migration from West Africa to northern Europe is affected by the Moon. These birds munch a lot of crabs, but during the spring new moons, fiddler crabs emerge from the mud to look for love. The earlier the new moon is in spring, the more crabs whimbrels eat, and the earlier they set off on their journey north.

The curlew's impressive bill is quite fragile, so it has internal struts to strengthen it. However, these don't leave much room for the tongue, so this is shortened. Female curlews have longer and more curved bills than males, and are better at feeding in soft mud.

PARENTAL PROTECTION

*Birds will resort to some unusual tactics
to keep their eggs and chicks safe.*

Fieldfares nest in large groups, with colonies spread over a wide area. When a large bird predator threatens the eggs or young, all adults in the vicinity gather together to dive-bomb the intruder. Nothing exceptional there, you might think – except that, as they dive, the fieldfares defecate repeatedly over the predator. Some raptors have been known to die as a result of such messy encounters with fieldfares.

The purple sandpiper has an amazing ruse to lure predators away from its nest. It becomes a lemming tribute act, flexing its legs to assume a crouching posture, then running erratically and making squeaking sounds. This remarkable distraction technique is known as a 'rodent run'.

Kentish plovers nest on wide-open sandy beaches, where it can get extremely hot. When an adult leaves the nest, it partially buries its eggs with sand to protect them from the fiercest rays.

Sandgrouse are birds of the desert. They lay their eggs in a shallow scrape in the middle of nowhere, far from a water source, as a form of protection. But they have a dry diet of seeds, so they – and their chicks – need a supply of water. The chicks are flightless for a month after hatching, so every day the male sandgrouse flies to a water source and dips its belly feathers in the water. These feathers are three or four times more absorbent than a sponge and become completely soaked. The male flies back to its nest and the chicks drink from the feathers.

Even with just one chick, the male guillemot's parenting burden is a heavy one. The chick leaves the ledge when it's only about 25 per cent grown, with poorly developed wings. The adult male may fly down at the same time, or call the chick from the sea. Either way, adult and young reunite on the water and swim out to sea, where the parent feeds and cares for the baby for at least a month.

FAVOURITE BIRD FACTS:
TREECREEPER

- Treecreepers often build their nests behind fragments of flaking bark.
- A treecreeper has a specially stiffened tail to use as a prop when climbing.
- Treecreepers are unique when it comes to the moulting process, because their outer tail feathers are replaced first and the inner ones last. This means the tail is always useful for climbing.

ALIEN CHECK-UP

*Birds are such a common sight that it's easy to forget
they're really quite alien creatures. After all, birds are
dinosaurs. Going even further back, birds are part of the
group Diapsids, which diverged from our own group —
the mammalian Synapsids — 318 million years ago.
It's no surprise that we don't have much in common!*

Birds have paired chromosomes, as we do, but the males
have two of the same (ZZ) and females have two different
ones (ZW). Human males have XY and females XX.

Birds don't breathe in and out like us, and they don't
have a diaphragm. Their respiration system is more
like a continuous loop, maintained by differentials in
pressure between air sacs throughout the body, especially
in their bones.

Birds see colour far more vividly than we do.

Birds don't sweat – imagine the mess that would make of the feathers!

Birds undergo some extraordinary seasonal internal changes that would be hard for us to cope with. For example, their intestinal tracts may greatly increase in length and size in the winter, to cope with the change from easily digested insects or worms to hard-to-digest seeds and nuts.

Birds may all but shed their sexual organs from autumn to mid-winter, when they aren't breeding. The gonads are of no use, so they regress to a fraction of their size.

Birds make their songs and calls with a special organ located where the windpipe divides into the two branches (bronchi) that go to the lungs, unlike our vocal cords, which are at the top of the trachea. Their location means that, with potentially two airflows, birds can sing two songs at once.

Swifts and hummingbirds have very short wing bones, which means that they effectively fly with their fingers rather than their arms.

Birds have four types of cone cells in their eyes (tetrachromatic vision), while we have three. Birds also have double cones, which detect luminescence. The cone cell type that we lack, but which birds have, is sensitive in the ultraviolet spectrum.

Eagles can see large objects five times further away than the average human, although not all birds have similar acuity.

ON CHRISTMAS DAY
IN THE MORNING

What's on the schedule for the average bird on a typical late December day? Spoiler alert – it's not very Christmassy!

First and foremost, in the cold midwinter a bird must eat enough to build up fat reserves that can take it through the long night ahead. A goldcrest – a bird that loses heat easily because of its surface-to-volume ratio – must spend all day foraging.

Many birds need to make foraging trade-offs, balancing the need to feed with the danger of predation. On very cold days, birds often have to take risks, feeding out in the open to get enough, despite being easier to detect.

Birds will often start their day by joining up with other individuals to form a flock. Flocks are mainly a strategy to allow for communal detection of predators.

Birds in flocks may need to establish or re-establish hierarchies. Some birds are simply bigger, stronger or fitter than their peers, and waste no time asserting themselves. A bird's place in the hierarchy can determine its prospects for survival, as it can earn itself better access to resources. A dominant greenfinch, for example, needs to store less fat overnight than a subordinate, because it has better feeding prospects.

A few birds will spend part of the day singing – it's only a few short weeks before they must have a territory firmly established.

The winter solstice has passed. Amazingly, birds will soon establish that the days are lengthening. They know this as light passes through the skull into the hypothalamus.

Most birds will take a bath sometime during the day. Experiments have shown that birds that have just bathed are more efficient at escaping from predators.

All birds must preen and maintain their feathers.

A bird may need to fight over its roost site. Or it might have to bed down with a large number of its peers at a communal roost. Starlings probably don't get much sleep!

A VERY SMELLY CHRISTMAS

*We don't associate birds much with smell,
but recent studies suggest that birds can smell very
effectively. (This may not be a good thing, as some
birds — especially seabirds — are also very smelly!)*

Albatrosses use a combination of sight and smell to find food on the open ocean. They are thought to use smell about 50 per cent of the time.

Great tits and blue tits detect chemicals given off by trees being attacked by insects. The trees 'call' to the birds to come and eat the offending animals.

In experiments on pigeons, it was found that blocking the olfactory sense impaired their ability to find their way home. Swifts and starlings are also impaired in finding their way back to nest sites if their sense of smell is experimentally removed.

We all love the smell of freshly mown grass, and it turns out that white storks do, too! The smell guides them to fields where prey might have been recently. In experiments, the storks homed in on fields upwind, which they could not otherwise see or hear.

Wilson's petrels follow scent trails to edible plankton by flying in a zigzag as they travel upwind.

Storm petrels use smell to recognise their partners, as each bird has a unique scent. House sparrows can also recognise their relatives by scent, which prevents inbreeding.

Black kites have individual smells, which change throughout the year. It is possible that pairs use changing smells from the preen gland to synchronise their reproduction.

Lesser black-backed gulls may use smell to correct their migration if they have gone off course.

Shearwaters can recognise their burrows by smell when they visit the colony in the dark.

Some larks put dung next to their nests in order to repulse predators with sensitive noses.

FAVOURITE BIRD FACTS:
SEDGE WARBLER

- Sedge warblers aren't reed birds, as you might expect – they prefer the adjoining scrubby bushes. Remember – 'sedges like edges'!
- Female sedge warblers are stimulated by a rich song repertoire. These creative males have a higher mating success.
- Male sedge warblers don't just sing on the perch, they also have a brief, lively song-flight. The healthier a bird is (i.e. the fewer feather parasites it has), the more song-flights it performs.

- Sedge warblers stop singing as soon as they are paired.
- This species migrates to West Africa for the winter. Before they leave, they all head to reed beds and binge-eat plum-reed aphids. This fattens them up enough to fly from northern Europe, across the Mediterranean, across the Sahara and straight to the wintering grounds.

GULLS JUST WANNA HAVE FUN

*Nobody seems to like gulls, but I think they
deserve a break. So here are a few facts about them
that will make you see them in a different light.*

Gulls are good at everything – flying, walking, running, swimming. They stand out among birds for being exceptional at all these things.

They are common around much of the world except the tropics, where it isn't windy enough.

The gull used for the introduction to everyone's favourite radio show *Desert Island Discs* isn't a real gull.

Many large gulls have orange spots on their bill in the breeding season. Newly hatched chicks are fed only when they peck at this spot.

Gulls often indulge in 'foot-paddling', where they seem to be dancing, or at least vibrating their feet in puddles. This behaviour is thought to imitate the movement of moles or raindrops, causing worms to come to the surface.

Gulls are famous for their confusing plumages. They moult twice a year and take some years to become mature – two, three or four years, depending on species.

PIRATES
(NOT OF THE CARIBBEAN)

We don't often think of birds as thieves,
but they cheat and steal all the time!

Pigeons steal food from much cuter birds at our garden bird feeders. Except it's not really stealing, of course – they're just taking what's there, unaware that it's intended for other birds!

Feeding stations in gardens are hotbeds of nefarious activity. Tits often wait for rivals to get food and then simply steal from them. Coal tits are repeatedly harassed.

Arctic skuas in Britain and the north-east Atlantic obtain almost all their food in the breeding season by stealing it from other seabirds that are returning to the colony. They will chase kittiwakes, Arctic terns, puffins and guillemots to steal their food. Great skuas often chase larger birds, such as gannets, but are also known to attack razorbills.

A family of seabirds called frigatebirds are piratic nuisances in the warmer oceans of the world.

Lots of birds of prey, including white-tailed eagles and peregrines, steal food from each other or other birds. Golden eagles sometimes steal food from foxes.

Common gulls share grassy fields with lapwings and golden plovers, mainly searching for worms, which the gulls incessantly steal from them. The gulls even divide the flock between them, with certain individual gulls having a 'territory' containing plovers to abuse!

Gadwalls steal food from coots. They wait for the coots to dive down for food, then seize it when the birds resurface with edible vegetation. Apparently, it's only gadwalls on the bottom rung of society (the subordinate individuals) who partake in such skulduggery.

FAVOURITE BIRD FACTS:
CAPERCAILLIE

- Capercaillie were extinct in the UK by 1780s. The entire population today stems from reintroductions since the 19th century.
- They're still incredibly rare in Britain, but these birds are common in Scandinavia. And there are about two million of them in Russia!
- The name translates from Gaelic as 'horse of the woods'.
- They sometimes eat snow in order to get water, and many individuals eat nothing but pine needles in winter. Some pine trees take a dim view of this and produce chemicals that the birds don't like, to keep them away.

SEASON'S GREETINGS –
WONDERFUL WARBLERS

*Enjoy a metaphorical moment with the sun
on your back as you contemplate the arrival
of warblers in the spring. It isn't far off!*

Chiffchaffs often sing from bare or dead branches near the tops of trees.

Once breeding is underway, chiffchaff pairs rarely meet up. The female builds a nest close to the ground, incubates the eggs and usually feeds the young on her own. She stays low down, while the male sings incessantly from the canopy.

The willow warbler is unusually violent in defending its territory, with a lot of fighting between males.

Female willow warblers are drawn to males with a high song rate – the chatterboxes, you might say.

The willow warbler is the only British breeding bird with two complete moults a year. Each one takes place in a different location – one in Britain and one in sub-Saharan Africa.

All willow warblers migrate to Africa for the winter, even those breeding in eastern Siberia. That's a 12,000km (7,456-mile) journey, which seems strange when they could simply slip down to the benign climate of southern Asia.

In continental Europe, wood warblers often change breeding sites from one year to the next. This behaviour seems to be related to the population of voles, as fewer of these ground-nesting birds breed when voles are abundant. The mammals may eat the eggs, or attract a higher density of common predators. Nobody knows how the warblers assess vole numbers.

The marsh warbler is Britain's latest breeding bird to arrive. Sometimes it doesn't arrive until June, by which time some species have all but finished breeding.

The rate of a male blackcap's song appears to give the female an indication of the quality of its habitat. Males with higher song output have richer vegetation in their territories.

The Dartford warbler often uses stonechats as sentinels when feeding. The latter are good lookouts, but they don't like the Dartfords following them!

Lesser whitethroats are unusual in that they winter much further east in Africa than most other British migrants, and take an easterly route through the Mediterranean. If you find a common and a lesser whitethroat in the same hedgerow in autumn, you know that in a few months' time they will be 3,000km (1,864 miles) apart.

FAVOURITE BIRD FACTS: GREAT TIT

- Urban great tits have higher-pitched voices than their rural counterparts, because the higher song is better for carrying above the sound of traffic.
- These formidable garden characters sometimes catch and eat small birds and even bats.
- During the egg-laying period, when the female is most fertile, the male great tit won't let her out of his sight in case her attention is drawn by a rival,

higher-quality male. As part of this 'mate-guarding', the male great tit sings loudly outside his mate's nest-hole at dawn and, at dusk, will accompany her home to roost. He remains on guard until it is dark.

FIRESIDE CHATS

*It's the season of cosy chats to pass the long
winter evenings, so let's have a chat about chats.*

Both stonechats and whinchats are about 12.5cm (5in) long,
but the wing-length of a stonechat is 65–66mm (2.6in),
while that of a whinchat is 76–77mm (3in). A whinchat's
wings are also more pointed.

Many stonechats don't migrate very far – or indeed, at all –
while whinchats migrate to sub-Saharan Africa. The
whinchat flies 300km (186 miles) extra per millimetre of
wing, compared to even the longest-migrating stonechat.

The stonechat's alarm calls, 'sweet' and 'sack', have different
functions. The 'sweet' call is to suppress the begging calls
of the youngsters, and the familiar 'sack' call is to draw
attention away from the nest.

Both redstarts and black redstarts have an odd habit of constantly shivering their tail. Nobody has yet proven why they do this.

A famous monograph of the redstart was written by John Buxton, who had been a prisoner-of-war in Bavaria during the Second World War. It was there that he first began to study the birds.

Black redstarts are often drawn to seemingly insalubrious places, such as industrial sites, dockyards and abandoned buildings. They build their nests high above ground, sometimes as high as 45m (148ft), and on ledges at the top of cliffs or buildings.

The black redstart is an indefatigable singer and may repeat its song 5,000 times a day, well into twilight.

One astonishing female black redstart laid 62 eggs in a 5-year period, and raised between 49 and 51 young.

Along with ravens, wheatears exhibit the largest altitudinal range of any British bird – from below sea level to mountaintops.

The wheatear migrates to Africa for the winter. Lots of birds do that, of course, but wheatears have a whole range of starting points. This songbird has spread all across northern Asia to Alaska, and west to Iceland, Greenland and northern Canada. The Alaskan birds migrate all the way across Asia and the Middle East and arrive in sub-Saharan Africa after a journey of 14,500km (9,000 miles). Meanwhile, birds from Canada fly across the Atlantic, sometimes on a single-leg stretch of 3,500km (2,175 miles). They then have to cross the Sahara to get to their wintering grounds. Despite their long journey, wheatears are among the earliest migrants to arrive back in the UK, often in very early March.

FAVOURITE BIRD FACTS:
KINGFISHER

- Adult kingfishers feed their young in a carousel system. The young form a ring, with their backs facing inwards and their bills outward. The hungriest youngster faces the light coming up the tunnel, gets fed and then everybody moves round.
- There is evidence that, after breeding, sibling kingfishers disperse together.
- The kingfisher is one of Britain's most productive birds, potentially bringing up three broods of six young every season.

LET'S MAKE PIGEONS POPULAR!

*Pigeons aren't the most popular birds,
but it's Christmas so let's give them a break.*

Collared doves have a song of three notes, which often sounds like a football chant: 'U-nit-ed!' Apparently, some males are so hopeless that they only sing two coos, not three. This doesn't help their mating success.

Pigeons suck! I don't mean this in a derogatory way – pigeons are among the very few birds that can suck water. Most birds only scoop up water, lift up their heads and let gravity do the work.

If you're planning any home improvements, don't enlist the help of a woodpigeon or collared dove. Their nest platforms are so shoddily built that you can often see the eggs from below.

Pigeons are unusual for only laying two eggs per clutch (a 'pigeon pair').

Have you ever seen a baby pigeon? No, I haven't either! They do exist, but they remain in the nest until they are the same size as adults, by which time they look so similar that no one can tell the difference.

Pigeons are highly sensitive to atmospheric pressure and may be able to tell when the weather is about to change.

CHRISTMAS NUMBER ONES

There are no particular categories, but here are a few
of my favourite birds that take a random top spot.

The great black-backed gull is the world's largest gull and the
little gull is the smallest.

The collared dove is perhaps the world's most successful
colonist. Once confined to India and Sri Lanka, it made its
way west and east under its own steam, reaching Europe in
the 1900s. From there, it colonised the whole continent in
about 70 years, conquering 45km (28 miles) every year. It
reached Britain in 1953, and there are now 795,000 pairs.
It was accidentally introduced to North America in 1974
and is now found in all the lower 48 states.

The peregrine is found throughout the world. It's an
inveterate consumer of feathered flesh and has almost
certainly eaten more species of birds than any other predator.

There's not a shred of proof, but could the siskin spend more time upside down than any other British bird? It almost always seems to prefer this position on feeders.

FAVOURITE BIRD FACTS:
OYSTERCATCHER

- Despite the name, oystercatchers rarely eat oysters.
  They much prefer other bivalves, including
  mussels, as well as worms and crustaceans.
- They have feeding 'guilds' that specialise in a
  certain type of hunting – mainly the 'hammerers'
  (brute force) and the 'stabbers' (guile and speed).
  Others probe the mud for worms or clams
  ('clammers'?).

- The hammerers are mostly males.
- Unlike most wader chicks, young oystercatchers can't feed themselves and instead have to rely on parental supplies.
- Youngsters learn to feed by watching their parents.

A WORLD OF BIRDS

As you've seen, British birds lead interesting lives,
but bird life can get even more bizarre when
you venture beyond British shores.

During the breeding season, eastern screech owls often
hunt for blind snakes, which they bring back to the nest.
Some of the snakes survive and feed on insect larvae that
accumulate in the nest litter. These larvae can be parasites
to owlets, so the presence of 'domestic' snakes is beneficial
to the growing young.

Scientists in New Guinea have discovered that some birds
that live in the forests there, especially pitohuis, are
poisonous. The toxin is similar to the lethal ones found on
the skin of tropical arrow poison frogs.

The crested auklet and whiskered auklets of the Aleutian
Islands have such a strong smell that you can detect their

colonies out of sight downwind. It's not an unpleasant odour, though – it's a bit like tangerine.

Australian swiftlets have an excellent answer to the universal problem of not enough childcare – the youngster incubates! A pair lays two eggs 50 days apart. The first hatches, grows up and incubates the second one.

The black-headed duck of southern South America is a cuckoo tribute act. It lays its eggs in the nests of other birds and never raises its own young. Its main hosts are another duck, the rosy-billed pochard, and two species of coot.

The maleo fowl of the island of Waigeo in Indonesia often lays its eggs in warm volcanic soil heated by geothermal activity, or on sun-drenched beaches. Eggs are laid 10–100cm (4–40in) deep in the sand and left to hatch on their own.

Splendid fairywrens and related species have a similar courtship display to humans. They bring flowers to their mate – or flower petals, at any rate.

BRITAIN'S LEAST
APPRECIATED BIRDS

You probably didn't buy this book to learn about the species below, but I feel they deserve their moment in the spotlight.

The word 'stock' refers to a tree trunk, so the name of the stock dove is appropriate, because this bird nests in holes in trees. They particularly like holes in beech trees on the continent because the smooth, slippery bark is thought to give protection against predators such as pine martens. Stock doves are also known to use rabbit holes for their nests.

Common gulls are the original 'sea gulls,' a term coined in 1544. Unusually for a gull, they often nest in trees.

Unlike many ducks, gadwalls are solidly monogamous. Ninety per cent of all females are paired up by November, many months before breeding takes place. Unpaired gadwalls spend more time swimming than paired ones. Work that one out!

Meadow pipits are unremarkable small brown birds, but they do have fans. Merlins love to eat them! These pipits are classic 'partial migrants'. Within a given population, some migrate to warmer climes and some don't. If the winter is mild, the remainers get the advantage of being on territory early. If it's harsh, more evacuees survive. Over time, the species as a whole prospers.

FAVOURITE BIRD FACTS:
GREAT CRESTED GREBE

- The nests of the great crested grebe can float, and may wash away if the grebe hasn't carefully attached it to some vegetation.
- Grebes cover their eggs with waterweed when they need to take a break from incubation so they can feed.
- For reasons that are as yet unclear, great crested grebes eat large quantities of feathers! This may help to swamp sharp fish bones in the bird's stomach.

- They have a very long breeding season. They may start in March and birds may be still be looking after their young in October.

THE BIRDSONG NO ONE
WANTS TO HEAR

We think of birdsong as beautiful and uplifting.
But not all birds are cut out to be singers!

The lovely 'shack-shack' flight call of the fieldfare is a
delightfully atmospheric winter sound. In summer,
however, this bird's song is truly horrible – a discordant,
fitful sound, lacking any musicality!

The spotted flycatcher's song barely deserves the name:
it's just a collection of high-pitched squeaks. Not one for
your playlist!

Pied wagtails 'sing' a bunch of calls bundled together in a
rushed fashion. It sounds like some kind of mechanical
implement in dire need of repair.

If a few spits and clicks float your boat, you might find a
modicum of charm in the hawfinch's pathetic effort. But

don't criticise a hawfinch's singing to its face – they're known to bite!

If you like your birdsong to be reminiscent of the noise of a dentist's drill, listen out for Savi's warbler.

CROWN JEWELS

We don't have many bird species unique to the UK or the British Isles. However, Britain and Ireland do have a few specials, mostly subspecies. The only species exclusive to Britain are the Scottish crossbill and the red grouse.

Most European common crossbills feed on spruce cones, but Scottish crossbills in Caledonian pine forests eat the local produce and have somewhat heavier bills than their common counterparts. Whether they are really unique to Britain has been hotly debated, and to muddy the waters, a Scottish crossbill was recently spotted in Paris!

The red grouse is closely related to the willow grouse (or willow ptarmigan), which occurs in Eurasia and North America. It differs significantly in that it does not go completely white in winter. In 2024 it was officially declared a separate species.

The pied wagtail is just one of the widespread white wagtail species. It's common throughout Britain and Ireland – but nowhere else. However, it has occasionally bred in the west of France, so if we'd managed to keep Normandy after the Hundred Years' War, it would be endemic!

Birds with subspecies that are only found in Britain and Ireland include bullfinch, long-tailed tit, black grouse and treecreeper.

We have two types of dipper – one of which is found in Ireland and the Hebrides, the other elsewhere.

The Irish coal tit is very different to the British coal tit – itself an endemic subspecies – by virtue of having yellowish cheeks (as do juvenile coal tits everywhere)!

Britain has a scattering of island races:

- The Hebrides has the Hebridean song thrush (which also occurs in parts of Ireland).
- In Shetland and the Outer Hebrides there is a subspecies of starling.
- There are separate wren subspecies on St Kilda, Fair Isle, Shetland and the Outer Hebrides (Western Isles).

FAVOURITE BIRD FACTS: YELLOWHAMMER

- Yellowhammers aren't summer visitors, as many people think – they're here all year. Up to 1,000 birds have been seen in a single flock.
- For a resident bird, the yellowhammer is a very late nester (not until May). It has a second brood in July, during which it feeds its young on plentiful grasshoppers.
- The yellowhammer's gorgeous colour is an indication of fitness. Females are drawn to the yellowest males, which are often the oldest birds.

- The birds with the brightest yellow plumage have the fewest parasites (lice, ticks and so on) on their feathers.

TV SHOWS WITH A TWIST

We all love a bit of Christmas TV, even if it's just re-watching some of the classics from yesteryear. But who would be the stars of the show in the world of birds?

MARRIED AT FIRST SIGHT
Starring: Pied flycatcher

Well, not quite first sight – a study showed that female flycatchers made an effort to get to know about six potential partners before deciding on one.

LOVE ISLAND
Starring: Seabirds

The TV show might have been inspired by the habits of birds – closely packed breeding-age individuals of the same species but the opposite sex. You've seen what happens!

BRITAIN'S GOT TALENT

Starring: Birds of prey

Let's amend the title to *Britain's Got Talons*. Most birds of prey kill using their sharp claws to rip through flesh, rather than their bill. The exception to the rule are falcons, which have an unusual edge to their bill that can sever their prey's spinal cord. Not family viewing.

A KILLER IN THE FAMILY

Starring: Swallows

Unpaired male swallows sometimes kill chicks in cold blood – they simply pull them from the nest and drop them to their doom on the ground below. These murderous males often pair up with the female whose chicks they have killed.

MIDSOMER MURDERS

Starring: Carrion crows

As 'murder' is the collective noun for crows, it's perhaps no surprise that the birds (as well as rooks) often feature in the soundtrack to the popular detective series. You can hear plenty of birdsong in the rural locations of the show, although it's not always accurate. If the producers are looking for birdsong consultants, we'd be happy to help!

STORAGE HUNTERS
Starring: Jays

Jays are the best-known caching species in Britain, storing thousands of acorns away every autumn. Many remain in the ground and eventually flourish into oak trees.

DIGGING FOR BRITAIN
Starring: Burrow nesters

Many birds dig burrows for their nests, including kingfishers and sand martins, both of which may construct their nest chamber 1m (3.3ft) deep. Puffins do, too.

NEIGHBOURS
Starring: Seabirds

Seabirds are long-lived and also faithful not only to their colony, but to their specific nesting site. They are likely to find themselves next to the same neighbours every year, and as birds are known to have different personalities, there are probably plenty of arguments!

NIGHTMARE IN SUBURBIA
Starring: Tawny owls

Tawny owls are extremely territorial – see one in your garden and you can be sure it's a long-term lodger. In the autumn, tawny owls will attack and kill any intruders in their territory, even their own chicks.

GEORDIE SHORE

Starring: Gulls

There are some delightful seaside locations near Newcastle and you can occasionally see a gull or two making a cameo in the TV show.